get
what you
want

get
what you
want

the art of
making and manifesting
your intentions

by
Tony Burroughs

BRISTOL PARK BOOKS / NEW YORK

First BRISTOL PARK BOOKS edition published in 2016

BRISTOL PARK BOOKS
252 WEST 38TH STREET
NEW YORK, NY 10018

BRISTOL PARK BOOKS is a registered trademark of BRISTOL PARK BOOKS, INC.

Published by arrangement with Start Midnight, LLC

Cover Design: Scott Idleman/Blink
Cover Photograph: iStockphoto
Text Design: Frank Wiedemann

ISBN: 978-0-88486-610-7

Printed in the United States of America

TABLE OF CONTENTS

· ·

Introduction by Brenda Knight ix

Preface by Tina Stober xv

A Friendly Note from the Author xix

chapter one YOUR POWER 1

Your Power, Inertia, The Downside of
Conforming, Sabotaging Phrases, Not Guilty,
Work, The Progression of Power, Getting
Unstuck, Flexibility, Steering the Storms, Getting
Extra Help, Positive Outcomes

chapter two THE ESSENCE OF INTENDING 31

Adventures, How to Think, Stating Intentions,
Desires, The Highest Good, Direction, A
Done Deal, Repetition, Speaking in the
Present, Conscious Language, Beginner's Luck,
Overcoaching, Patience, Keep Moving Forward,
Waiting, Tolerance, Discerning, The Ideal Deal

chapter three THE CODE 75

Inside the Code, The First Intent – Support Life,
The Second Intent – Seek Truth, The Third Intent –
Set Your Course, The Fourth Intent – Simplify,
The Fifth Intent – Stay Positive, The Sixth Intent –
Synchronize, The Seventh Intent – Serve Others,
The Eighth Intent – Shine Your Light, The Ninth
Intent – Share Your Vision, Creating Your New
World, The Tenth Intent – Synergize

chapter four UNIVERSAL TRUTHS 115

Relating, Multitasking, A Higher Point of View,
Projects or Problems, Looking Within, No
Secrets, True Communication, Receiving Your
Own Messages, Grace, A Story from the Past

chapter five MONEY AND MANIFESTING 143

Opening, Abundance, The Big Warehouse,
Embracing Upliftment, Your Calling, Speaking in
the Positive, Meditation, Inviting

chapter six LOVE AND GRATITUDE 163

Higher Priorities, Learning to Love Better,
Getting Home, Finding Your Heart, Gratitude,
The Bigger Picture

chapter seven **RELATIONSHIPS** 179

The Highest Good Again, Negative Emotions,
Backbiting, Renewing, The Children

chapter eight **NATURE** 193

Our Mother Earth, Nature, Beauty, Dramas,
Ceremony, Common Sense Revisited

chapter nine **ADVERSITY** 213

Staying Uplifted, Doubts, Balance

chapter ten **LETTING GO** 221

Growing Up, Illusions, Window-Shopping,
The Old Ways and the New Ways, Integrating,
Treasure Hunting

chapter eleven **FREEDOM** 239

Freedom, Expanding, Freeing Our Spirit, Global
Observance Day

chapter twelve **HEALING** 253

Wellness, Confirmation, Lumping, Shining Light
and Sending Love, Becoming Less Suggestible,
Devices, Aging

chapter thirteen **PEACE** 277

The Good Side, Our True Heroes, Mercy,
Nationalism, Setting an Example, Good News,
Positive Language, Your Inheritance, Timing, The
Godspark, The Marriage of Mind and Matter,
Peace

chapter fourteen **ONENESS** 313

The Magical Flow, We Are All One, Community,
Networking, Projections, The Power of the
Circle, The Intenders Circle, The Intenders Circle
Format, Some Common Questions, About the
Intenders, Your Next Step

chapter fifteen **FINALE** 339

A Pop Quiz, "The Bridge" Messages

The Code 363

Introduction by Brenda Knight

All editors believe in the books they pick to publish. But it is rare for an editor to claim that a book completely changed their life. In this case, as Associate Publisher and founder of Viva Editions, I am here to tell you that Tony Burroughs's teachings on the art of Intending may have even saved my life or, at the very least, my sanity. I still remember when I first touched the envelope containing Tony's manuscript. It was the end of a long and fruitfully busy day but I was feeling a little guilty about a stack of book proposals awaiting my attention in the white post office bin beside my desk. I sorted through them quickly, the "yes, no, and maybes" practically organizing themselves when I finally got to the last envelope in the bin. When I touched it, I felt a frisson of excitement. I immediately knew there was something there. I was excited and settled in to read whatever it was that contained the energy that sparked through a padded manila envelope. Fascinated, I read about Tony Burroughs and how he came to this wisdom. Suddenly, it was made so clear to me that I could use "intention-setting"

as a way to improve my life, a rudder with which to navigate its vicissitudes.

Little did I know how much I would need the wisdom of Intending and just how soon.

Tony's own story reads like fiction. He moved to Hawaii and became a farmer of exotic fruits, no less. The Elder who was training him to grow fruit in the middle of the Pacific was rather exotic himself, given to pronouncements of esoteric philosophy. As Tony was mastering fruit farming, he was also, unknowingly, being carefully mentored in a deep and ancient spiritual wisdom. Fairly quickly, Tony and three friends held the first "Intenders Circle" in Hawaii. It was nothing short of miraculous. In fact, one of the three, Tina, was even "bringing through" the teachings of Lee Ching.

If channeling is news to you, as it is to many, the concept itself is quite old: an ascended master, one who has passed from the earthly realm, can pass information "through" a channel, someone who will speak their messages out loud. Lee Ching had much on his mind and conveyed many important messages through Tina to Tony and the Intenders Circle. Lee had come from an ancient time of war and strife and very much wanted to speak of how people today can live in peace and harmony with Intending as a central tool. Tony and the Intenders took this as their mission—to share the art of Intending as well as other deeper, more eternal wisdom.

It was close to midnight but I called the number on the

submissions letter. Tony answered and we got a book deal rolling.

No wonder I could feel the power through the envelope. Electrified, I told everyone who would listen about my new discovery—all my friends, coworkers, even a VP at Barnes & Noble who said, "Oh, it's like *The Secret* but real and for the highest good of all, without the self-centeredness."

At the time I was happily ensconced in a relationship and a home. My partner of fifteen years and I finally decided to invest in a house with a teeny tiny view of the Pacific Ocean and room for my gardening projects. About a month after I first met Tony, we were hit with hard news. My partner, Robert, was diagnosed with very serious health challenge. Our world was turned upside down. Unfortunately, Robert's illness was advanced by the time it was found so it was only a few short months from diagnosis to his death. I felt like I lost everything.

It all happened so swiftly that I was in shock, barely able to function. Nevertheless, I needed to function more efficiently than ever; Robert had no will because we thought he had months or even years to live. His estate was put into probate and I was stuck with a mortgage built for two on a slim salary for one. I quickly used up all my cash on the mortgage, memorial arrangements, etc. Then I got into the credit card trap, cash advances at a penurious interest rate, every mistake in the book you can make. I remember thinking to myself, "I will become one of those women who lives in her car, the working homeless." I kept a lot of this a secret and did my best to hang on.

As financially poor as I was, I have always been rich in friends, and some of my girlfriends compared notes and figured out I was cracking under the pressure of all the debt. Grief-stricken, I was broke and my spirit was breaking, too. Amanda, a mom with a new baby and a brilliant mind open to new ideas, suggested we try that "intending stuff" I used to talk about all the time. We gathered up an Intenders group of three, just like the early Hawaii days for Tony. I brought in a crudely copied version of Tony's instructions for setting up an Intenders Circle and we got started. It was a relief to talk about what I needed to set Intentions for, even though it was somewhat overwhelming. I needed:

to sell the house and get out from under the mortgage;

to find a new home that was affordable, nurturing, and right for me;

and to make more money.

As you'll learn from these pages, it's best to state your Intentions specifically, in clear, positive language. As long as it's for the highest good of all, you can get what you want.

Amanda wanted a certain kind of bookcase for her baby's toys and baby books. Billee wanted a writers' group and a good and interesting job. So, here's the kicker—I wanted a new home I could afford with a basement, a view, a fireplace, and a garden. For the highest good of all. We had our first lovely little Intending session and went our separate ways.

The next day, Amanda called me, "You're never going to believe this. I walked outside my house this morning and at the end of the block someone had left a virtually new bookcase exactly like I wanted. Wow!"

I was amazed but a little doubting voice in my head said, "No way you can sell that house and find a rental you can afford with a view, a fireplace, and a garden. No way!" I ramped up my Intending and started each day off with stating my Intentions aloud and also visualizing them.

We kept meeting and our Intenders Circle in San Francisco became the highlight of the week for us all. Billee got into a writers' group and got a fantastic new job. Each week, new reports of highly successful Intending occurred.

Finally, I got an offer on the house I needed to sell at a modest profit but with one caveat: I had to be packed and out of the house in two weeks. I had nowhere to go. Maybe I was going to live in my car after all.

I added a nightly Intending session as my bedtime "prayer." That day I saw an interesting Craigslist ad for a place in the East Bay in my (low) price range. I went to see it the next morning at 11:11 and it was *exactly* what I had Intended for. I shocked the landlord by saying "I'll take it!" Flustered, he informed me there were a lot of people ahead of me that had already handed in credit reports. I ran down to the copy store a few blocks away and printed out the best of my three credit reports, all of which were about to bottom out. I raced back and handed him my report along with a freshly typed memorandum saying that I was looking for a peaceful home in which to write and edit. That seemed to find favor with the owner.

Two days later, upon learning that I'd never smoked a cigarette in my life, he rented me the place. I'll never forget that moment of joy: I had a new home that suited my needs to a tee.

But, it was not exactly as I had Intended. It was better! My new home had a basement plus a big old garage and two views: one of the Golden Gate Bridge and one of Mt. Tamalpais! There was a front yard and a backyard with two terraced, landscaped gardens. Best of all, there was a fireplace in the living room and one in the backyard, too. I took one look at the fireplaces and knew they would be the gathering places for my friends and the site of many Intenders Circles to come.

After that, there was no stopping me. If you say hello to me, I will probably start evangelizing about the success I've had making and manifesting my Intentions. I feel honored to be a part of bringing *Get What You Want* to the world because I know this book contains great truths that can help us all.

I Intend the best for you and yours and for us all.

Brenda Knight
El Cerrito, California
October 2012

Preface by Tina Stober

I am Tina Stober, one of the four original Intenders of the Highest Good, and I feel so privileged to have had the opportunity to have a friend like Tony Burroughs in my life. Tony is a seeker, hungry for information to change his own life, the lives of his friends, and people everywhere.

For those of you who are new to *Get What You Want*, allow me to shed a little light on the subject for you. Originally called "The Bridge," it is a series of a hundred and twenty revolving daily messages that Tony brought out on the Internet a few years ago at www.intenders.org. Currently, with tens of thousands of subscribers around the world, it has become one of Tony's greatest gifts to his fellow men and women.

My involvement in all this came about because I have been a medium for an amazing being named Lee Ching for over twenty-five years. When we started the Intenders seventeen years ago, Tony encouraged me to bring Lee Ching out to speak to our group. I did that and have been involved in giving readings for Intenders and friends all across the country ever since. During this time, Tony, Lee Ching, and I enjoyed many private sessions together as well. These sessions were always wonderful because Tony used them to gather deeper insights and information for the purpose of helping himself and helping others through his writings. (As a point of interest, Lee Ching is responsible for bringing through many of the italicized "one-liners" under the title headings in each of these messages. They came directly from the channeling sessions held after our early Intenders Circles.) I think it takes a visionary to think forward like that—to tirelessly go for the gold, to listen and be able to hear what is most relevant to our times and bring it forward. It is simply amazing!

Many people in my readings have said, "I read Tony's messages every day and they have been so meaningful in my life...it's like they speak to me personally as if each message was just for me." I tell you true that these are timeless messages, and I thank God someone had the forethought to share them with thousands of people online. And now I thank God again that Tony has taken these wonderful messages and compiled them into a book that will touch even more people around the world. I, Tina Stober, personally thank him for being the scribe for Lee Ching, an awesome, loving being wanting so much to be heard. My gratitude goes out to you, Tony, for your thirst for knowledge, a thirst that we are all benefiting from.

Now Lee Ching has something to add:

"In these times, especially when so much fear is being generated by a few and believed by so many, these positive words and insights capture the hearts of those who deep down know the truth and yet need to get agreement somewhere for their inner knowing. Blessings are flooding now to those who have been using what they have learned from these Get What You Want/Bridge messages about creating their own reality. Now you are creating a reality that is much better than the one the media would have you believe in because you are remembering that your life is a clean slate for you to write on. You need to be different to make a difference.

Many blessings are coming to those of you who are grateful for what is in your life at this moment. Gifts are being given, as well, to those who have learned the laws of manifestation. And much love is filling your world now, overcoming hatred and war. It is a wave of love and healing that you, by your thoughts, have created.

Tony, I am so happy that you have taken these messages of love out to the world in every way that you can—through your books, your DVDs, the use of these profound messages, and your monthly Intenders newsletters. I applaud you for keeping the good word going out. Your vision for the world is becoming a reality with a capital R.

To the lucky ones who will read this work compiled and written by Tony Burroughs, I say this: read, practice, and live your life fully and freely from this moment on. My blessing reaches out to this work of Art and to all those who find joy and benefit from it.

Much Love,
Lee Ching"

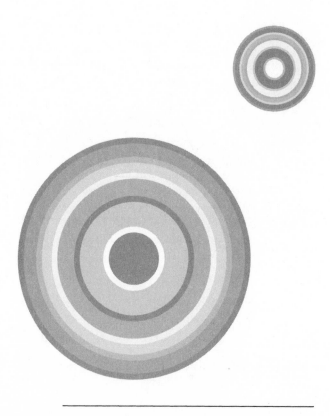

A Friendly Note from the Author

Get What You Want is not your typical book. It is not meant for you to read from cover to cover like most other books, although you can do that if you like, and many people do. No, *Get What You Want* has been purposely set up to awaken something magical and mysterious within you—and all you have to do to make it work is say a quick intention, open it to any page, and it will tell you what you need to know.

The old English word for this process is "bibliomancy," or book magic, and it calls upon us to suspend our logical, established ways of thinking for a short time in order to make room for our intuition to awaken. Using *Get What You Want* as a magical tool will give you clarity and guidance for whatever is going on in your life at any given moment. Of course, there is one hitch. You have to believe it will work. If you believe it will work for you, it will. On the other hand, if you don't believe, you might as well take a walk. In other words, you must trust in it, and if you do, the rewards are great, indeed, for you will tap into a huge part of yourself which has long been in slumber and awaiting your call.

Here's how it works: Pick up this book and hold it for just a moment. Take a breath or two, let your thoughts settle, and be open to receive. At this point, you can either allow the book to hone in on the perfect message that is for your Highest Good, or you can pick a situation in your life that you'd like clarity or resolution on. Then say, "I intend that everything needing to be known is known here today and that the messages and guidance I receive from this book are in total alignment with my Highest Good, the Highest Good of the Universe, and the Highest Good of everyone concerned." Then, open the book to any page and start reading.

Be assured that the message you receive is the one that is best for you in the moment. These messages have been tried and tested by thousands who have signed up to receive them daily from our www.intenders.org website, and the remark we hear most often from our subscribers is that the message they received that day was the exact message they needed most in their life at that time.

That having been said, it is my intention that you test *Get What You Want* for yourself and that you use this magical book to avail yourself of all the wisdom, joy, love, and abundance that the Universe has to offer.

Tony Burroughs
September 2012

chapter one

YOUR POWER

YOUR POWER

*What you are looking for
is what you are looking with.*

GET WHAT YOU WANT WAS CREATED TO ACT AS a way for you to move, as easily and effortlessly as possible, from the mainstream to the magical. It will bring your level of personal empowerment up to speed so that you can have a positive effect upon your world. It is also designed to help you gain a degree of proficiency in using the Laws of Manifestation or the Intention Process (as we call it), so you will no longer remain as easily controlled by others—others who may or may not have your highest and best interests at heart.

Get What You Want has been purposely set up to do three things at the same time: first, to empower you to reach your highest potential; second, to demonstrate the great benefits in coming together in community; and third, to act as a guide for The Code so that you reawaken your conscience and begin to love, honor, respect, and care for your fellow travelers once again.

And that is our intention for you—for you to take these tools and do what you came to this beautiful, abundant Earth to do. We congratulate you for having the courage to take these steps into your own power. Now, as we prepare to offer you *Get What You Want*, we leave you with these few words of encouragement...

"Your joy walks with you every step of the way. You need look no further than that which is your own Being. The world would have you think otherwise, and yet, what you do, how you think, and what you feel is entirely up to you. You are truly a magnificent entity with powers lying dormant and feelings, so sublime, ready to burst forth like a young flower, which spreads its petals for the first time to greet the morning summer sun.

How long will you wait before you see yourself in your highest light and do what makes you truly happy? What will it take for you to open your heart and radiate outward the ocean of love that lives within you? You have been bound up too long, shackled to your fear, imprisoned by ghosts who are not real unless you make them so. The world needs you to be happy, to shine your light on all that you see, to laugh without limit, to touch the hearts and minds of every man, woman, and child who come your way.

Take a chance now and live life like you've always wanted. Envision yourself throwing off the fetters of fear, and calling unto you the glory that is yours by right of birth. Let your joy blaze like a fire in the night. That's what the world needs from you. And, more than that, that's what you need from you."

MY INTENTION FOR TODAY IS:

I Intend that, from this moment forward,
you and I and all of the people
we come in contact with,
and all of the people they come in contact with,
and all of the people they contact—
until it fills the entire Earth—
live in utter joy and peace.

INERTIA

Everything we put our attention on
becomes more, bigger, and brighter.

Inertia is the force that keeps something or someone who is moving in motion, and it keeps something or someone who is resting at rest. In order to overcome it and have something new happen, a special kind of influence or energy is necessary. In terms of the quality of our lives, we'd have to care a lot more about our world than we've cared in the past. We'd need to start moving in a different direction. This is what The Code does, for embedded within its lines is the promise of a better life for all who are willing to think something new.

If you sit in on the average casual conversation today, much of the talk would likely center around the national picture, what the politicians are doing, and where "we" are headed. You and your friends would probably agree that the national situation isn't giving you what you really want; that you seem to have lost your freedom, your peace, your own power to do with as you please; that our war-like tendencies simply aren't serving us anymore; that our distribution of goods and natural resources favors the "haves" and penalizes the bulk of the world's people; that you live in fear; and so forth. You could go on and on listing the flaws in the current system, and almost everyone would have an opinion that would ostensibly help to make things better from within the framework of the current system. The current system, however, is first and foremost an illusion that we choose to keep our attention on. We could just as easily talk about something else, if it weren't for the power of the inertia we keep bumping into. Just try to get your friends to set the topic of politics aside for a while, and see what happens. In most instances, it would be as if no one heard you. They'd keep on talking, lost in the inertia of the national collective mind.

There are those who would say that we're powerless to make changes in the face of collective inertia, but this simply isn't true. As we said earlier, changes occur when a new influence or energy is introduced into the picture. So, let's shift the inertia by introducing The Code into our hypothetical scenario. We'll apply the Ninth Intent and make an intention around it by saying, "I Intend that I am creating my ideal world by envisioning it and telling others about it. I share my vision." When we do this, our imagination is unleashed. We have a new direction, one that gives us the autonomy to create our own vision, and the knowing that, in the envisioning, we are actively and consciously creating something better for ourselves. Our power instantly returns to us, and, from this point on, we're back on track, doing what we came here to do.

MY INTENTION FOR TODAY IS:

*I Intend that I always have enough
to spare and enough to share.*

THE DOWNSIDE OF CONFORMING

*Don't forget: Your purpose on Earth is to evolve
to your highest possible state of being.*

From the time that we were small children, we've been taught to mind our manners and to be like everybody else. We're told that it's respectful of others to practice certain courtesies, and that's fine, as long as we don't become slaves to what other people think or say about us. Taken too far, our conformity keeps us living in a subtle, but very real, state of fear. We become afraid of acting differently than everyone else around us. Even when our heart tells us to do something one way, our social consciousness screams out to do it another way, lest we draw too much attention to ourselves. And all too often, our fear wins out.

To experience your highest light, you must break the mold. You must do things not as others do, but as your heart bids you to do. Put on your old comfortable, raggedy clothes and take a walk around the park; whisper to a flower in your backyard; get up at four in the morning and go out and take a look at the pre-dawn skies. There are those who might contend that you're ready for the loony bin. But they'll be the ones who are missing out on some of the finest experiences in life. They'll stay under the thumb, albeit unconsciously, of others who would control their every word and deed. While you, in your newfound wisdom, will begin to walk this Earth freely and fearlessly, without a care in the world.

Know that there will most certainly be times when you'll feel the pressure to conform from those all around you. Just remember, in these moments, that it is you, not them, who gets to sing as you amble through the beautiful park. It is you, not them, who hears the joy in the voice of the flower as she whispers her innermost secrets back unto you. And it is you, not them, who receives loving guidance from the morning star as she breaks the horizon at dawn.

> **MY INTENTION FOR TODAY IS:**
> . . . .
> *I Intend that I am my own person.*

SABOTAGING PHRASES
. . . .

What you say is what you get.

The Intenders of the Highest Good understand that the exactness of our words counts. We know, beyond all doubt, that the words we are using are constantly determining the kind of experiences we will have. By the same token, we have become more aware of when we are projecting an experience out into our world that we really, in our hearts, do not desire to see manifested. People do this unconsciously in their everyday conversation quite often. We call it negative projection or self-sabotage, and we gently point it out to each other when it happens in an Intenders Circle.

Much of the time, these self-sabotaging words and phrases are added onto what we have just said, like an afterthought. For example, you'll frequently hear someone say, "I intend that the repairs go easily and effortlessly, *without too many problems*." By adding on these last four words, they've suddenly undermined their original intention. They've sabotaged their own future by bringing *problems* into the picture.

When we Intenders catch ourselves projecting an undesired experience like this, we immediately remind ourselves of one of the main reference points in the Intention Process—that our thoughts and our words are constantly creating our world. The old saying, "As you believe, so it shall be for you" is a great truth. Since our words are exact reflections of what we believe, it is prudent for us to be much more careful with the words we are using. It's simply not in our highest and best interests to continue to be frivolous with our words. These words have power. They can either limit our experience or enhance it.

Here are twenty self-sabotaging phrases that we've heard recently. You can make your own list too, just by listening closer to what you and the people around you are saying.

1. There's never a place to park when I need one.
2. Why is everything always so difficult for me?
3. Some things never change.
4. There's no possible way this is going to work out.
5. It's too late.
6. I just can't lose any weight.
7. It's going to be too expensive; we'll never be able to afford it.
8. So-and-so is incapable of changing; they're a lost cause.
9. It doesn't look very promising.
10. Easier said than done.
11. Well, I'll be damned.
12. It's going to be a bad allergy season this year.
13. I'm afraid there's not going to be a good harvest this year.
14. The weather is getting worse.
15. I'm just real sensitive to those things.
16. There's nothing we can do about it.
17. What a struggle this is.
18. This is a pain in the neck.
19. I'm getting sick and tired of all this.
20. The doctor says it won't go away.

MY INTENTION FOR TODAY IS:

. . . .

I Intend that I am clearly shown what I am creating with my everyday thoughts and words.

NOT GUILTY

. . . .

Let not your heart be troubled.

Perhaps one of the greatest challenges that faces the average person today is believing in their own self-worth. From the time we were small children, our view of our highest light has been undermined. It's pretty easy to recall past experiences where we've been told that we were less than we thought we were or that we'd made a mistake. Our teachers, parents, peers, the TV, and all sorts of sources have, either consciously or unconsciously, talked us into limiting ourselves. Over a lifetime, our power was slowly but steadily stripped away from us. But now all of that is changing.

These teachings emphasize that you've never made a mistake. When the incident occurred where you thought you'd made a mistake, it wasn't until after the incident was over that you gleaned the knowledge from it. While the incident was still in progress, you were only operating on the basis of the best information that you had at the time. In truth, you couldn't have known any better and, therefore, there was no reason for you to beat yourself up about it. You were presented with a lesson, but no mistake was made.

Learning a lesson and making a mistake are two entirely different things. Lessons don't carry the same feelings as mistakes. There's no guilt attached to our lessons, but mistakes imply that we've done something wrong. Those who view life from a higher perspective know that they've never done anything wrong. Everything just happens and it doesn't serve us to place moral judgments on any events that occur in our lives. The concept of right and wrong is simply another illusion that doesn't exist for us unless we nourish it. We can choose to plead not guilty to all of the menacing should haves that charge us with wrongdoing. In our mind, we can assert that everything is all right regardless of what others may say, and, in doing so, we return to the innocence we were born with.

Each person is responsible for his or her own happiness. You needn't feel guilt or obligation in regard to other people. It isn't your fault if you inadvertently made them unhappy. They are only relating to you according to their own past experiences and their own processes.

Truly, it is not someone else's decision as to whether you are a good or kind or loving person. If you and your soul intend to be good and kind and loving and gentle, and even if you are those things and others don't see it, it's their shortsightedness. It is not you.

MY INTENTION FOR TODAY IS:

I Intend that I am always seeing myself in my highest light.

WORK

Your work is meant to be enjoyable for you and helpful to others.

One of the downsides of remaining in a state of disempowerment is that we are often relegated to spending our days doing things we don't really like to do. The idea that we can't have the job we truly want runs rampant through our world, causing so many to drive long distances or to subject themselves to unhealthy working conditions for eight or more hours a day. In short, our entire view of how we look at our work needs an overhaul. But interestingly, the overhaul that's needed isn't apt to come from the top down; the employers of the world are steeped too deeply in the status quo for us to expect them to make any drastic changes. The overhaul must come from the bottom up; it must come from you and me, standing firm and trusting that if we are to have a job that's both enjoyable for us and helpful to others that, as we Intend it, it will make itself available to us.

> **MY INTENTION FOR TODAY IS:**
>
> *I Intend that the work I am doing is both fun for me and practical for others.*

THE PROGRESSION OF POWER

The reality that you create is up to you.

Anyone who desires to become more proficient at using the Intention Process must pass through six stages or steps before becoming an adept. I was fortunate to learn these steps from a tall, highly intelligent man who mysteriously showed up at my doorstep one summer day when I was living in Corrales, NM. He said his name was Ralph, and that he was an author of a different sort than me. Whereas I'd always been interested in the intuitive side of life, Ralph's talent, as I soon realized, was that he was scientifically oriented. He liked to analyze things and put them in order.

After a few minutes of customary introductions and niceties, we got to talking about the laws of manifestation, and Ralph said that, lately, he'd been writing about something he'd discovered in his research. It had to do with a particular progression that most people go through in order to become more skilled at manifesting.

The initial step in this progression, he said, was testing. If we're going to create anything consciously, we must first run a test by making an intention and establishing for ourselves that the process works. Once we realize that our intention has, in fact, manifested in our physical experience, we'll be more apt to test it again by making several more intentions and watching closely for them to manifest as well. In this way, he said, we gain a modicum of proficiency and work our way toward the second step in the progression: we begin to trust.

Ralph explained that the more we see our intentions come

into manifestation, the more our level of trust grows. We start to get comfortable with the process and, usually not long after that, we reach the third step, which he called confidence. Confidence, according to Ralph, comes to us when we understand that we're really on to something. At this point, we typically begin using the Intention Process more often. We use it to bring anything that we need into our lives, and we use it confidently.

After noticing that our intentions are coming to life on a steady basis, our confidence then turns into a knowing. This is the fourth step, and Ralph said that this is where our manifesting skills take a gigantic leap. He said that in preparation for the book he was currently working on, he had interviewed hundreds of people and found that those who had a knowing about their ability to create consciously lived an altogether different kind of life than those who hadn't reached this stage yet. They had a charisma about them; they'd come in touch with their innate power, and, from this point on, there was no turning back. He said it was as if they'd awakened from a dream and had no desire to go back to sleep. Life had regained its excitement and adventure, now that they had accessed their true power. The only thing left for them to do after that was to act courageously. And that is the fifth step: courage.

When we reach the stage of courage in our evolution, we are no longer hampered by what others think or say about us. Fear and intimidation don't play the same roles in our lives as they used to. We call forth the Highest Good and make our intentions courageously, knowing that whatever we're intending is going to manifest for us.

Our base of power grows stronger and stronger, and soon, after acting with courage for a while, we reach the sixth and final level on our journey: fortitude. We become like a castle or an impenetrable fortress built upon the peak of the mountain. Having made our way through the previous five steps, we stand firm, at the pinnacle of life, masters of all we survey. Nothing can touch us now. We are grand creators, freed from all worldly cares as God's most precious gifts are arrayed before us to pick and choose from as we please.

MY INTENTION FOR TODAY IS:

*I Intend that I am a Mighty Manifester
and that all good things come to me
easily and effortlessly.*

GETTING UNSTUCK

Let your thoughts know that you are in charge.

Did you ever notice that you'd be listening to a song on the stereo and for the next several hours or days the same lyric keeps running over and over through your mind? Or when things get a little hectic in your life that your thoughts tend to turn dark and repeat themselves like a tape stuck in an endless loop? Sometimes that's the Universe's way of getting us to see something about ourselves that we may have been overlooking. But, most often, it is simply our ego mind or unfriendly invisibles parading our worst fears before us. In either case, we need to learn how to deal with it.

After setting intentions that I am guided, guarded, protected, and that I am serving the Highest Good of everyone involved, I slung my new backpack over my shoulder and walked into the forest. In seconds, the canopy enveloped me, and I couldn't tell north from south, or east from west. The only thing I could do was keep moving forward. The voices in my head came loud and insistent right away. They said I was crazy, that I could die out here without ever having helped Trish or Mustafa. They said to watch out for wild animals, quicksand, poisonous water, and more.

It reminded me of something Kokopelli said, in between all the dancing and merry-making. He said that our mind is like the barker at a carnival, and then he cupped his hands like a megaphone and started shouting, "Come one, come all! Come every thought imaginable. Step right up and I will view you. I will give you energy and attention." Then he uncupped his hands and continued, saying that most of us allowed the barker to go on indefinitely, even though we knew, deep down, that everything we put our attention on gets stronger.

According to him, it was up to us to ground our thinking, and, whenever our thoughts were flying here and there, we needed to see ourselves, and others, in their highest light, whole and perfect, and let our thoughts know that we're in charge. When our thoughts get out of hand, like rowdy children, we should tell them, "Get behind me! Leave me be! I have no use for you! You are only holding me back! I have an opportunity in this life to be a God/Man, to become master of my fate. I will not listen to you one minute longer. I will not be swayed by your trickiness."

Finally, after having had as much of this negativity as I could tolerate, I screamed, "Leave me alone! Get behind me!"

Much to my surprise, that worked. My mind stilled, and I suddenly became more aware of the beauty of the forest. As my breathing deepened, the glow around the branches and rocks appeared and, with each step, I found myself slipping into another world.

> ### MY INTENTION FOR TODAY IS:
> . . . .
> *I Intend that I am commanding*
> *my negative thoughts to go away.*

FLEXIBILITY
. . . .

You can, at any moment, transmute your karma.

We, as human beings, tend to think that our destiny is set in stone; that we are stuck in an endless loop of experience after experience leading to who knows where. We've been told that we set "causes" in motion long ago and we must live out the effects of those causes in our daily lives whether we like it or not.

There's only one problem with this line of thinking. It is a limitation and we have come here at this time in history to rise above all limitations and to express ourselves fully.

So, how do we transmute our causes? Well, for openers, we Intend it!

You are learning that once you intend something, and it is in your highest and best good, it will make itself available to you. If, however, you are still believing in fear or suffering more than you believe in the Highest Good, you will be experiencing more of that.

We limit ourselves immensely when we think that things cannot change. In truth, change is the one constant in the Universe that we can rely on. There is nothing we cannot change, even our karma.

MY INTENTION FOR TODAY IS:

I Intend that I am an unlimited Being.

STEERING THE STORMS

You are more powerful than you know.

When you get a lot of people agreeing and envisioning the way things will be, then that's the way things will be. There is tremendous power in a group of people focused on a common objective. It works within a positive environment, such as in an Intenders Circle where everyone is holding a vision of everyone else's intentions being manifested; and it works just as easily within a negative atmosphere, such as when we're creating fearful weather conditions for ourselves.

You don't have to look very far to see that our weather is being tampered with. Those in power would have us believe that the weather is out of our control, that we are at the mercy of the storms and climatic changes, but this simply isn't so. In fact, it's just the opposite. It is we who create every aspect of our environment, including the weather. We've just forgotten about it.

So, here's a gentle reminder. Night after night, in homes all across the globe, the weathermen and women prance across the TV screen telling us what the weather is going to be like. Much in the same way that the drug companies create flus and sicknesses of all sorts by describing them and pulling flimsy "facts" out of thin air, the weather people describe the coming weather changes, and, if we believe them, we add to the creation of the bad weather.

Can you imagine the power in that? Millions of people holding the same thought is an awesome prospect in itself. And now, with all the satellite imagery graphics, the friendly weatherperson can even have us picturing large weather systems impacting whole parts of the planet. This is the point where we give up our power and hand it over to someone else. People everywhere either forget or simply don't realize that their thoughts are creating their world. They buy into the pictures they see on TV and waste no time telling everyone they run into that a storm is on the way.

That's how storms, flus, or any other mass events are orchestrated. And if that isn't enough, now the weather people have even created "seasons" for the storms and sicknesses in order to get us primed and ready to experience bad times. Is there anything we can do?

Yes. Two things. First, we can withhold our agreement every time someone tells us a storm is on the way by simply refusing to believe it. In that way, we are not adding to or reinforcing the event.

And second, we can become proactive by using the satellite images against themselves. Whenever we see the great masses busily creating a storm, we can become a Storm Steerer. Instead of believing that a hurricane, for instance, is going to follow the course described by the anxious weatherperson, we can use the wondrous light-working tool we call our imagination, and, in our mind's eye, we can Steer the Storm out to sea, or see it dissipating into nothing before it has a chance to hit land.

Now...what if enough Storm Steerers pictured the storms going away? They would go away. I've seen huge tropical storms move away from the Big Island after fifty Intenders "intended" it. Can you imagine what would happen if thousands of people from all over the globe became Storm Steerers? It would change everything, not just with the weather, but with the way we create our entire world.

Freedom. This was the teaching of the Native Americans. Surrounded by the blackness of night, they danced around the campfire, whooping, hollering, yelping. This was their show of freedom, in sounding it outwardly to the world, in sounding it into the vast silence that was all around them. They shouted fearlessly into it. And the hills would reflect it back...it was like a miracle.

> **MY INTENTION FOR TODAY IS:**
>
> *I Intend that I am refraining from buying into any media hype surrounding mass events, and that I am only envisioning positive outcomes for the Earth and her people.*

GETTING EXTRA HELP

You can ask your angels to talk to their angels.

How many times have you been in a situation where one of your good friends approached you with a drama that was seemingly hopeless? They had no idea how to proceed and no one to turn to. Perhaps it had even been going on for quite awhile with no resolution in sight. Perhaps, also, you had told your friend to make some intentions around the drama, and yet, because of their doubting nature or inexperience at manifesting, they were still up to their neck in the quicksand of the situation. In short, nothing was working.

When we're in situations like this, where we really want to help someone else, but don't know where to turn, this is what we've learned to do. We go into our quiet place where we will not be disturbed, and we ask our angels to talk to their angels.

I was staying with friends recently who had no idea where their next mortgage payment was coming from and it was driving them crazy. They didn't quite have the handle on their doubting and so they kept inadvertently sabotaging their intentions by saying, over and over, that they really didn't want to lose their home. It was like a broken record, and even though I pointed it out to them on several occasions, they still weren't able to keep from voicing their doubts.

The only thing I could think of to do was to have a talk with my guides and helpers in the invisible realms and petition them to talk with my friends' angels and helpers.

Now it is several months later, and I can't tell you exactly how it all worked out, but I do know that my friends are still living happily in their home and that all of their payments are up to date. The only thing I can attribute to this once seemingly hopeless situation is that our unseen helpers—our angels—took care of everything.

> **MY INTENTION FOR TODAY IS:**
>
> *I Intend that I am helping to resolve my friends' dramas by asking my angels to talk with their angels.*

POSITIVE OUTCOMES

No one else can tell us what to think unless we let them.

When we realize that what goes on inside of us is our business and our business alone, only then can we begin to hold our own power. Of course, there are many people who, for their own selfish interests, would do their level best to tell us what to think and how the world works, but ultimately the reality we create for ourselves is up to us. Likewise, it serves us well to remember that what goes on in our internal world need not be dependant on what's going on outside of us. In other words, there could be all sorts of chaos and craziness going on around us, but if we're filled with happiness and joy on the inside, then we're happy and joyful, and everything else can stay on the back burner.

Of course, that's not what's happening in the lives of most people nowadays. Most of us are attached firmly to our outer world and continue to make things worse for ourselves by dwelling on our doubts, dramas, and disasters, not realizing that we are creating or reinforcing these things when we do so. If, instead, we would become more vigilant of our thoughts and words and then begin to place our attention on more positive outcomes, then that is what we would start to manifest for ourselves.

It seems to me that one of the biggest barriers to really being of service to others lies in our tendency to "dumb down." You know what dumbing down is, right? Dumbing down is when we act like we don't know what's going on because we're afraid of others who appear to be more powerful than we are. It's when we're timid and don't say anything at times when we actually could have a positive influence on the situation. That's what I was doing.

I remember one specific time when I was sitting in a coffee shop with a group of friends, and one guy was saying that there really isn't any such thing as God, and that this reality here on Earth is the only one there is. This man was very strong-willed, and I didn't say anything. I dumbed down, even though I'd had several mystical experiences, and I knew that God exists.

Later on, after I got home, I thought about what we'd talked about, and something didn't feel right. There were several young people there that day, and they were starting to believe the fellow who was so powerful. I could have served them by saying something to balance out his persuasive, but misguided views. But I didn't. So I intended, right then and there, that I would never miss an opportunity like that again.

Since then, I've come to understand that it doesn't serve anyone if I allow others to have their way just because they're more eloquent or more persistent than I am. I speak my truth, and now people don't run over me like they used to. My life, on a personal level, works so much better now that I've stopped dumbing down. Come to think of it, I'll bet our whole world would be a better place if more of us would stop dumbing down and speak out for what we truly believe in.

MY INTENTION FOR TODAY IS:

I Intend that I am at peace within myself.

chapter two

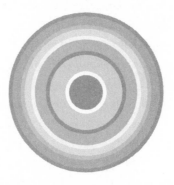

THE ESSENCE
OF INTENDING

ADVENTURES

You are being taken to places where you are needed.

DURING THE PROCESS OF WRITING *GET WHAT YOU Want* I've had to be a guinea pig of sorts as I put these inspiring messages to work in my own daily life. After all, what good would they be if they haven't been tried and tested? In other words, I've had to walk my talk, and this has taken me to some surprising places along the way.

There are too many stories to tell all of them here, but suffice it to say that I started out by writing the first thirty messages last winter at home, in my little office, overlooking the snowcapped Rockies in the Four Corners region of Colorado. About that time, with the temperature dropping toward zero, my wandering spirit got the best of me and I took off down the road, not knowing where my next stop or next dollar was coming from. All I had was my '95 Dodge van and my trust.

After a few days in Tucson with my close friends, Tim and Victoria, I headed west to the coast for some beach time and, as I was driving across the southern Arizona desert, I got a call from my friend, Brenda, in San Diego, who happened to mention that her sister had a place there that was empty, if I was interested. I said yes and the next day, after sleeping in the van that night and bathing at the beach showers in La Jolla, I drove up to Escondido where Brenda's sister lived. The house turned out to be an estate with all the trimmings! Fifty acres of avocado trees, a huge pool and Jacuzzi, and all the fruit I could eat.

I ended up staying there over a month, writing in the mornings and driving to the beach in Encinitas every afternoon. Then one morning I received an email from an Intender up in the hills above LA, and the long and short of it was that she and her husband were in the movie business—he is a successful screenwriter and she turned out to be an actress I'd seen on TV—and they invited me to come and visit with them and present a workshop for their friends.

Feeling a little foolish for even considering leaving the lavish mountaintop estate in Escondido, I packed my things and drove north to Topanga Canyon. For me, this was just too synchronistic to pass up because my guidance had told me many times over the years that I would be making movies of my books and workshops.

It turned out that my new friends lived in a mini-castle atop a gorgeous mesa above Topanga Canyon on a seventeen-acre ranch. After presenting my workshop, they invited me to stay longer so I could continue my writing. In short, it was paradise. I became part of the family and got to walk the magnificent beach at Malibu every afternoon. While I was there, I continued to write.

Toward the end of my stay in Topanga, I started getting phone calls from Georgia and Florida asking if I would like to present workshops there. I agreed and called my girlfriend, Vicki, and she joined me for the remainder of my time in California. She even brought along my Manx cat, Puddy, and the three of us decided to make an adventure of it all (as if it wasn't adventurous enough already) by camping at several beaches before driving across the country.

As you can see, life was good, even though we still never quite knew where our next resources were coming from. We were told to do what we loved to do and to spend what we had and it would be replaced, perhaps from sources we hadn't even expected. So that's exactly what we did. We camped, ate at the little beach shacks along the coast, and had a blast! The high point for Vicki was one evening at sunset when we sat next to Matthew McConaughey at an outdoor seafood café in Malibu.

Our travels then took us across the country to Atlanta for a Humanity's Team conference and down to the southern tip of Florida by way of Disney World and Universal Studios. Camping and staying in Motel 6s (because they allow cats), we ended our tour by traveling up the east coast to visit Vicki's mother in the heart of Pennsylvania Dutch country in Reading, PA.

And that's where I am now, living on the side of beautiful Mt. Penn, looking out at its mystical Pagoda that sits, like a throwback from another world, at the top. I've written another three dozen messages here and, in three days, we head up to Canada for more workshops, and then back home to Colorado.

Anyway, I thought you'd like to know what's been happening to me as a result of putting these teachings to work in my life. I can tell you that from the mountaintop estate in San Diego, to the crystal mines of Arkansas, to the water-slides at Universal Studios, Florida, it has been a wonderful ride. So far, everything I've needed has come to me, and if the abundance of grateful emails I've received is any indication, I've helped a lot of people along the way. Admittedly, there were times when I didn't have the slightest idea how we would come up with the money for gas or a motel room, but these things always appeared, although sometimes at the last minute. The only guideline I'm following is that I'm doing what I love to do and living my calling at the same time. As a result, my life is a constant adventure, and now that I've gotten used to it, I wouldn't have it any other way.

Now, all I have to do is keep intending, letting go of my old ways, and stay connected to the Highest Good. The Highest Good seems to want me to have a grand time, and so far, so good. If, however, it turns out that I end up working the night shift in a pizza place somewhere on the outskirts of Durango, that'll be okay too.

MY INTENTION FOR TODAY IS:

. . . .

I Intend that I am following my calling
and doing what I love to do
at the same time.

HOW TO THINK

. . . .

The time is coming when you will have
a thought and it will be there.

The first reference point we adopted when we started the Intenders over a dozen years ago was that our thoughts (and our words) create our world. We knew that the key to our greatest happiness, as well as our gliding as gracefully as possible through these times of great change, lies in our thinking processes. Once we fully understood that our thoughts are the building blocks of our future, we realized that the solutions to any challenges we were faced with are not going to come through political or worldly means, but through our becoming more vigilant of our thoughts. We simply needed to learn to hold our attention on the thoughts that serve us and discard the ones that don't.

You see, from the time we were small children we were taught what to think, but, in all our years of schooling, we were never taught how to think. That's why we Intenders created the Intention Process. And that's what we're talking about—how to think—because another thing we've begun to notice recently is that the time between the time we make an intention and its manifestation is getting shorter and shorter. Therefore, it behooves us to keep a much closer eye on what we're thinking (and what we're saying) than ever before.

I recall an occasion last year when a friend of mine and I were pulling into a large parking lot early one Saturday evening to rent a video. Every space, for as far as we could see, was filled. Normally, we would have made an intention on the way to the video store by saying something like, "I intend we have a great place to park when we get there." Then, we'd invoke the

Highest Good and say, "So be it and so it is."

But we forgot to do that, and as we looked around and I almost started to voice a complaint, she suddenly remembered, then quickly stated an intention, said "So be it" and just as she did, a brown conversion van backed out of the space directly in front of the main door to the store. I got so excited that I yelled out, "And there it is!"

She pulled into the spot and both of us sat there laughing. Our "So be it and so it is" had turned into "So be it and there it is." We'd had a conscious instantaneous manifestation, and it was as if we'd received a confirmation that we were evolving to our next step. I can't tell you how good it felt.

> ### MY INTENTION FOR TODAY IS:
>
> *I Intend that I remember that what*
> *I am thinking and talking about all day long*
> *is what I am manifesting for myself.*

STATING INTENTIONS

. . . .

That which you are reaching toward
is also reaching out toward you.

The Intention Process is just about as simple as it can be. All
you have to do is say "I intend" and then follow it up with
whatever it is that you desire. It could be anything! You could
intend to have a new coat for yourself or you could intend for
world peace. Since there are no limits on what you can think
about, there are no limits on what you can intend!

For me, I get up every morning and I intend that I am joyful and
happy. I intend fun and laughter. I intend that I am in perfect
health—rejuvenated, aligned, balanced, and feeling physically
great all of the time. I intend that I am always guided, guarded,
and protected. These are a few of the general intentions that
I start with every day and then I look around at my life to
see what I am needing. If the old wheelbarrow just broke, I'd
intend that I have a new one. If the computer decided to go on
the fritz, I'd intend that it gets fixed. I don't leave anything out
because there's no reason to hold back!

I like to make a few intentions each day about my personal

traits. Sometimes I intend that I am a more compassionate person; or I intend that I'm more kind or gentle. And sometimes, especially when there are a lot of dramas going on all around me, I intend that I see everyone in their highest light and every event from its highest point of view. That way, I'm able to observe all of the sorrow and suffering in the world and still remain uplifted. I intend that I remember that it doesn't do anybody any good to drop down into someone else's challenges and become troubled or sad along with them. It's much better to set an example by staying happy and cheerful.

After intending for things like this for a while, I take a closer look at the world at large and make a few intentions for it too. For example, I intend that men, women, and children everywhere experience grace. And I intend that peace and harmony blossom all across the land. And I intend that this Earth is living in its highest light, and that, within our environment, the air we breathe is clean and crisp; the water everywhere is crystal clear and delicious; the soil is abundant with lush growth and beautiful fruit is dripping from the trees; the animals are honored and respected; and people all over the world are happy and smiling because they're being given everything that they need! And, last but not least, I intend that all of my thoughts, words, and deeds serve the highest and best good of the Universe, myself, and everyone, everywhere.

So be it and so it is!

> ## MY INTENTION FOR TODAY IS:
>
> *I Intend that I remember to start out every day by saying my intentions.*

DESIRES

*You can have anything and everything
you could possibly dream of—
even a whole new world to live in.*

Our desires help us set our course in life. The second reference point with which we started the Intenders was that our desires are in us to be fulfilled. Our guidance told us early on that we came into this lifetime with a certain set of desires and the way for us to know that we are evolving to our highest potential is by either transcending or fulfilling our desires. If we were born in an eastern culture, where spiritual pursuits are honored more, we might go into a monastic cell and spend anywhere from twenty minutes to twenty years meditating and transmuting our desires in order to get to what the Buddhists call a state of desirelessness. But in our western world where consumerism is king and we've been barraged by advertising since day one, we are probably best off to learn how to fulfill our desires. That's where the Intention Process comes in. We can learn to manifest our desires one at a time until there aren't any more of them.

It's interesting that in the west we have been taught to sweep our desires under the rug; that there's something wrong with us if we have desires. The Intenders' teachings remind us, however, that the word "de-sire" comes from Latin, meaning "of the Father," and that there is a sacred aspect to our desires. All we need to do to evolve and to empower ourselves at the same time is become more proficient at fulfilling them.

"When I arrived at my first Intenders Circle, I was homeless. I'd been trying to find a way to scrape up enough money to rent a small place, but things just weren't working out for me. I was getting desperate!

My friends who took me to the Intenders Circle told me not to hold back. They said that, at an Intenders Circle, "the sky's the limit," and that I should ask for my heart's desire. I made an intention to find a place of my own where I would be very, very happy and I asked that it come to me freely and easily.

It wasn't two days later and a lady who had been at the meeting called me and said she was going abroad for at least three years. She'd thought about selling her house, but it was such a lovely custom home, right down by the beach, that she couldn't bring herself to part with it. Maybe she'd be back someday, but, in the meantime, would I be interested in caretaking it for free?"

—KAREN REID

MY INTENTION FOR TODAY IS:

*I Intend that I am looking within
to see what would give me the most joy,
and then I am consciously creating it.*

THE HIGHEST GOOD

*What you are calling your
Intentions for the Highest Good
are the threads of the cloth being woven
into the robe of peace.*

In the Intenders, we don't have any rules, but we do have one thing that we never compromise on. It's what binds us together and we call it our "Highest Good clause" or "the world's greatest insurance policy." It works like this: when we make an intention—any intention—we always say that in order for it to manifest that it must serve the highest and best good of the Universe and the highest and best good for ourselves and everyone concerned. It's as simple as that! Oh, and by the way, even if we forget to say it, it's understood that the Highest Good clause is always in effect when we make our intentions.

> "When we first started to use the Intention Process, we thought that the only thing we were doing was learning how to manifest things so we'd be happier. It wasn't until we'd been at it for well over a year that we realized something else was happening. Not only were our dreams coming true, but we were also letting go of old stuff that we'd been hanging onto forever. It was that old stuff that was holding us back from living in our highest light. On one hand, our desires were being fulfilled; and, on the other hand, we were giving up our old desires that hadn't manifested. Pretty soon, we noticed that we didn't have as many desires as before. They had all either been manifested or let go of. That's when things started getting really good! We began to feel lighter and freer. The Intention Process was lining us up with our Highest Good, and what was being

brought to us was a more wonderful, much grander gift than we had received from the small, mundane intentions that we had manifested since we first started. It was as if we were sprouting wings."

—SALLY MOORE

MY INTENTION FOR TODAY IS:

I Intend that I am aligned with the Highest Good in everything I say and do.

DIRECTION

Surround yourself with people who are supportive of where you are in your life now.

After sitting in hundreds of Intenders Circles and watching thousands of Intenders make and manifest their intentions, we've come to realize that those who get up in the morning and set a direction for their day by saying their intentions, prayers, or affirmations have an entirely different experience than those who don't. They are becoming more conscious and they are not at the mercy of people or forces outside themselves like most people.

Instead, they are beginning to open the door to their own power.

Likewise, people who get together with a group of like-minded and lighthearted friends on a regular basis and put their intentions and gratitudes in a circle have an entirely different week than those who don't. Everything just comes easier for them.

> "There really is power in an Intenders Circle! My car threw a rod last summer when I was in between jobs. I made an intention to have another car come to me free, since I didn't have any extra money at the time. Four days later, my son called me up and, before I could say anything, asked me if I knew anybody who wanted a car—a nice, older, but sporty VW. He said that it was taking up too much space beside his carport, but that it ran great. And, it was first-come, first-serve. Within an hour, I caught a ride to his place, started up the car, and drove it away.
>
> It felt like Christmas in July!"
>
> —WAYDE CAMERON

MY INTENTION FOR TODAY IS:

*I Intend that I am creating a world
that is always in support of me.*

A DONE DEAL

. . . .

See the end result from the beginning.

When we are able to firmly hold a picture in our mind of that which we intend to create, and we reject any ideas that would interfere with that image coming to us, we are well on our way to becoming a Mighty Manifester. We make the very best use of the wondrous tool that we call our imagination. For it is here, within the vast, infinite scope of our mind's eye that we can picture anything. We can envision things that will help us and further us along life's path, or we can envision dramas galore. Both are equally at our beck and call. If, however, we are to put our imagination to its highest and best use, we will need to hold fast to envisioning positive outcomes and trust that they are manifesting for us.

Those of us in the Intenders who have been testing this method for the last several years can assure you that seeing the end result from the beginning—and remembering that our thoughts are the forerunners of our experiences—works. This is how we utilize our imagination to become more proficient at the fine art of manifesting. And the nice thing is that we don't have to go anywhere. From the time we make an intention, all we have to do is be open to receive.

My closest friend and longtime Intender from Albuquerque, Dave Powell, said it best. He treats all his intentions as if they are "a done deal." As he tells it, he makes his intentions and then lets them go, acting, from then on, as if they have already manifested. This system is obviously working because when I met Dave he had all sorts of financial challenges, but now he is as secure as anyone I know. And this is not because of an abundance of money (which he has created anyway), but because of his knowing that whatever he sees as "a done deal" really comes to life.

> ### MY INTENTION FOR TODAY IS:
>
> *I Intend that I am putting my imagination*
> *to its best use by holding*
> *a vision of my ideal outcome.*

REPETITION

. . . .

The Universe is user-friendly.

One of the questions we get asked the most is "How often do I say my intentions?" As we talk to people across the country we find several schools of thought with differing approaches to this question. Some say to state your intentions twice a day: in the morning, when you get up, and in the evening, before going to sleep; some say to state them once and once only; while the Intenders' teachings suggest that you say them once a day, preferably in the morning so that you can set a positive direction unto your day.

In weighing all of the various options about how often to say our intentions we've come to realize that all of them are right. You can say them once only, once a day, or twice a day. If, however, you are saying them more than twice a day—that is, you're saying the same intention over and over throughout the day—it implies that you are dealing with some doubts that you need to take a closer look at. You're not truly letting go and trusting in the Intention Process, and therefore, you'll actually be keeping your dreams from manifesting by the constant repetition of your intentions.

One evening in Leilani we were enjoying the thirty minute spiritual guidance session that followed our weekly Intenders Circle and we asked Lee Ching, our favorite guide who speaks through Tina, about how often we should be saying our intentions. He told us that it depended on how far along we were in our spiritual evolution. Those, he said, who are new to intending and self-empowerment will often say their intentions more than once a day and, even though they're still running doubts, the Universe will rally to their side just to make sure that they get some "wins" and become more confident in the process of manifesting. He said that the Universe wants to help anyone who is willing to make their intentions in the name of the Highest Good, and It will see to it that their first few intentions are manifested, even though they may still be harboring some doubts on a subtle level.

In regard to saying our intentions once a day only, he said that this practice had been used with great success since the days of old, and that it works for everyone no matter what stage of development they're in.

Then, he added something very interesting. He told us that, even though we may start out by saying our intentions daily or more, we will ultimately come to a point where we only need to say them once, and that's all. He said that it is oftentimes difficult for beginners to trust in this, not having had the experience of several "wins" under their belt, so, for most people, saying our intentions once a day works just fine.

"You can't go wrong by saying them once a day," he said, "but you will come to a time when you say them once only and know that the Universe heard you and is taking care of everything from that moment on."

MY INTENTION FOR TODAY IS:

. . . .

*I Intend that, with each Intention
that manifests for me,
I am building greater and greater
trust and confidence
in the magical workings of the Universe.*

SPEAKING IN THE PRESENT

. . . .

*Everything in your world—the world at large,
as well as your individual world,
including everything you see, hear, smell, taste, touch,
and feel—
is the result of a thought manifestation.*

When you first begin to form your intentions into words, it's always best to take a moment and create a very clear picture in your mind of that which you truly desire to manifest. See yourself in the picture acting as if it has already happened. Then you can use the words "I intend that I am..." and know that you've gotten off to an excellent start with your intentions.

Another phrase we've recently gotten rid of is "to be." In our Circles, we say, "I intend that I am happy," for instance, instead of saying, "I intend to be happy." This small but very important change has produced extremely rewarding results for us. It brings everything into the present time, as opposed to keeping our desires somewhere off in the future. There is a big difference in intending to be happy and intending that you are happy now. By intending that you are happy now, you are seeing the end result from the beginning. Otherwise, you can intend to be happy and the Universe may follow your exact instructions and keep you in a state of readiness for a very long time, waiting to be happy. If you don't rephrase your intentions, you could easily remain on the brink of your happiness indefinitely without ever quite reaching it.

Sometimes it also helps to imagine that you are working hand in hand with your guides, helpers, or angels from other realms, and that these helpers are there to serve you. They listen closely to your intentions and go scurrying throughout the far corners of the Universe, taking the thoughts and words that you have provided and then delivering them back to you down here on Earth in the forms and substances that you call third-dimensional experience. When you state your intentions in the present and envision them as if they have already occurred, you send the clearest possible message out to your helpers. You've made their job a lot easier, while optimizing your own potential for bringing your dreams into physical reality.

MY INTENTION FOR TODAY IS:

*I Intend that I am always phrasing
my intentions in the present tense.*

CONSCIOUS LANGUAGE

*Know that you are assisting others by your own
realizations. You then enhance and increase the
possibilities for others to go where you have been.*

Much of our lives have been spent thinking that we can be frivolous with our spoken words, but now we're finding out that it's to our great advantage to be clear and concise about what we desire to manifest. We know that our words are the building blocks of our future. With this in mind, we've eliminated five words that kept us disempowered and no longer serve us well. In our Circles, we've stopped using *trying, hoping, wanting, to be,* and *not* because they were interfering with the manifestation of our intentions. Today we will talk about the first three of these sabotaging words.

We eliminated *trying* because it's a halfway word. It provides a built-in excuse to be unsuccessful. If you're having a conversation with someone and you say, "I'll meet you tomorrow morning at 11 o'clock," and their response is, "I'll try," it isn't very reassuring.

We've also dropped *hoping* and *hopefully* from our vocabulary. When a person is *hoping* that something will happen, he or she is holding on to a little bit of doubt about whether their intention will really come true. If they replace "I hope" and "hopefully" with "I intend," and really trust in the Intention Process, then things will begin to change for them. They will stop limiting themselves unknowingly.

Wanting is another word that we refrain from using in our Intenders Circles because it implies that there is a scarcity of things. We looked it up in the dictionary and it said that if we were in a state of wanting, then we were lacking. So now, instead of saying, "I want a new car," we say, "I intend that I have a new car." This slight change, though very subtle, has taken scarcity out of the picture and brought us much closer to our own empowerment. (While we refrain from using the words *want* and *wanting* when we are stating our intentions, we realize that the average person equates their "wants" with their "desires." Hence, we entitled this book *Get What You Want* so it would appeal to, and have the chance of helping, the greatest number of people.)

You can easily tell what's going on in the lives of your friends and acquaintances by listening closely to what they're saying. If they are using these disempowered words, then they are most likely creating scarcity and limitation in their lives. You can help them to raise their level of consciousness by setting an example for them and, when they're receptive, by gently explaining to them how their words are limiting their experience. When you do this, everyone is uplifted. And that upliftment radiates outward into your community and into the world you live in.

MY INTENTION FOR TODAY IS:

. . . .

*I Intend that I am only using words
that serve me.*

BEGINNER'S LUCK

. . . .

*As soon as you see things in new way,
with a perspective of gratitude
and an opportunity for growth,
you will be rewarded immensely.*

One evening in our spiritual guidance session Tina was talking about invisible influences like emotions, cell phone frequencies, TV and radio waves, and so forth, which surrounded us. She also said that our Intenders Circles always had invisible Beings who gathered around us and that these helpers saw to it that the newcomers first few intentions were manifested very quickly and in such a way that they couldn't be missed. She jokingly called it a "beginner's luck factor" and said that we should tell those who were new to our Circles not to hold back, but to "go for it" and expect that whatever they were intending would come to them easily and effortlessly. Later, she also told us that it was not really luck at all, but a law, which calls forth special help from the invisible realms to rally around anyone who chooses to dedicate their intentions to the Highest Good.

> "I always had a knack for working on computers. When my friends would raise their hands in the air and threaten to bash their computers, I would offer to fix them. I'd been teaching part-time in the evenings, but I really wanted to be working full-time fixing computers. I also had a desire to be able to make low-cost secondhand or rebuilt computers available to the people in the area. The only problem I had was getting parts. I wasn't in a big city where parts were easy to find.
>
> About that time, I happened to go to an Intenders Circle. That night I made an intention to leave my teaching position and somehow, some way, start my own business fixing and rebuilding computers. Four days later, a friend of mine told me about a place where I could put a bid in on a whole container-load of good computer parts—CPUs, keyboards, printers, everything, including the monitors! I got the bid and, within two weeks, I rented a wonderful warehouse in town and stacked it full of all kinds of computer equipment. Everything I'd intended to have was right there at my fingertips!

Before I knew it, people were lined up at my door needing help with their computers. And when I'd help them, I couldn't resist also telling them about the Intenders."

—AARON CHRISTENSSON

MY INTENTION FOR TODAY IS:

I Intend that I am open to receive from both expected and unexpected sources.

OVERCOACHING

Ceremony allows people to remember who they really are.

We learn as we go. From our beginnings, the creation of the Intenders has been an organic process. Since we all believed that it was important to have a strong foundation before we put the walls and roof on a house, we have tested the principles set out in our teachings over and over in our Intenders Circles, and we have not hesitated to adjust or change something if it wasn't working for us.

We often talk about "What you say is what you get," and,

of course, that is true and very literal. How we approach this piece of information in our Intenders Circles, however, has shifted dramatically.

In the early years of the Intenders, we used to interrupt whoever was saying their intentions anytime they'd say, "I'll try," or "hopefully," or one of the other self-sabotaging words or phrases we talk about in The Intenders Handbook.

We don't do that anymore (with the occasional exception of casually clearing our throat when an experienced Intender continually uses one of these disempowering words), and here's why. First of all, it slowed down the rhythm and flow of our Intenders Circle. When we "overcoached" or corrected people all the time, our Circles tended to go on too late into the evening, and people began to get fidgety.

Second, over time we realized that people, especially newcomers, didn't want to be corrected on every little thing they were saying. We had several friends who were very interested in what we were doing, but our overcoaching seemed to frustrate them and they didn't come back to our Circle. Obviously, the way we were doing things was having the exact opposite effect from what we were looking to achieve.

And third, after we stopped being so persnickety about the exact wording in our Circles and allowed people to continue on with their intentions without interruption, we found that they started correcting themselves! With a little practice, we discovered that as our new Intenders began to get comfortable within the supportive atmosphere of the Circle, they also gradually refined their own speaking habits and eliminated the words that weren't serving them. We didn't have to say a thing!

So, nowadays, we don't correct anybody unless they specifically ask for it. We let them state their intentions and gratitudes without our interference—and now everything is a lot more fun.

So be it and so it is.

> ### MY INTENTION FOR TODAY IS:
> . . . .
> *I Intend that I am setting an example for others simply by being more aware of what I am saying.*

PATIENCE
. . . .

You know you need to learn patience when things are coming to you at the last minute.

Things can come to you at the last minute. In fact, you know that you need to learn patience when things are coming to you at the last minute. There is an interesting story sent in recently by my friend Pat in Canada that exemplifies this all-too-common scenario. Pat received it from her good friend in Hawaii who is living close to the land.

> "Years ago, in an entrepreneurship class I was taking, there was a woman who wanted to establish an emu farm. She and her husband read all the books on emus, on gestation time, and at what moment the chicks would hatch. They had a whole bunch of eggs they were incubating. At one point they figured the babies should be emerging, and, thinking nature had screwed up, took it upon themselves to crack the eggs and release the chicks. (I couldn't believe she actually told us this, I would have been so ashamed.) Needless to say, the baby emus all died. When you know that what you want is coming, don't interfere! That story still makes me shudder."

We in the Intenders have all had to deal with patience issues at one time or another, and the way we resolved them was to intend that we always have a "buffer zone" so that things come to us well before they were needed. Needless to say, we also had to learn to let go of our tendency to set time parameters and realize that the Universe often had different ideas about how long something was going to take than we did.

But once we began to see our buffer zone intention work, our impatience lessened and we relaxed because we learned that everything is coming to us in its perfect, right timing.

> **MY INTENTION FOR TODAY IS:**
>
> *I Intend that I have a buffer zone so that things come to me well before they are needed.*

KEEP MOVING FORWARD

Our challenges are there in order to take us to a greater awareness.

There are times for all of us when life presents its challenges. We might feel like we've lost our way and there's nowhere to turn. Every road appears bleak, cold, unforgiving, and the voices of doubt won't give us a moment's rest.

The Intenders would like to give some encouragement to those of you who are going through your stuff. When all hope appears to be gone, your intentions are still there. Your choices are still there. Keep moving forward. Even though the voices in your head tell you that all is lost and that any further action on your part would be futile, don't give up. Remember the truth: just because your intentions haven't manifested yet doesn't mean that they're not going to manifest.

Keep moving forward, no matter what. And intend that, from now on, all of your changes are gradual, gentle, and full of grace.

The Intention Process never fails. It is only when we become impatient, intolerant, or forget that our thoughts are creating our experiences that we bring suffering to ourselves. There is no situation that cannot be turned around. There is always a bright side. In every experience, there is a gift, even if we have to use a magnifying glass to find it. We can manifest miracles as long as we never give up on our dreams, as long as we intend it and keep lining ourselves up with the highest that is within us.

Be good to yourself. Life's experiences are meant to move us closer to realizing who we truly are. Every challenge takes us nearer to a knowing that, at our core, we are Spiritual Beings. And, always remember that things can change. Good things can happen in the blink of an eye. One moment you may be mad at the world and thinking about giving up on all that is near and dear to you, and, in the next moment, a spark of love may warm your heart and bring newfound joy into your life. Your Spirit may soar. Keep moving forward.

MY INTENTION FOR TODAY IS:

*I Intend that I am always moving forward
toward the manifestation of my dreams.*

WAITING

Things can come to you at the last minute.

The French have a word *denouement* which, in essence, means that sometimes we are taken to the eleventh hour and fifty-ninth minute and fifty-ninth second—and then the Universe lays everything we intended in our lap. Of course, we tend to think that we can second-guess the Universe by predicting the times when our intentions will manifest for us. But the truth is that we can never really know when things will happen. We can only know that they will happen.

Another thing I always admired about Mark was his relaxed attitude toward life; how he worked hard, but never seemed to be in a hurry. When I asked him how he stayed so calm, he said that he didn't allow himself to get too attached to specific outcomes, especially where time was concerned. He said that letting go and patience go hand in hand, and that we need to understand that our timing and the Universe's timing are two different things. Our manifestations, he said, really can come at the last minute. But, if we interfere with the Intention Process by doubting, cutting corners, or stressing and striving, we lose the chance of seeing what would have happened if we'd waited a little longer. In fact, he said, as hard as it is to get used to, there are times when it's definitely in our Highest Good to have things come to us at the last minute. How else, he asked, would we learn about trust? How else would we gain the inner strength necessary to take the next step in our evolution? He said that the Universe knows the precise, perfect time for the cocoon to open up so that the young butterfly can spread its wings and fly away. According to him, it's the same with us. But, like the butterfly, we must be willing to wait.

So often human beings sabotage themselves by not trusting that the Universe will bring their creations to them in the perfect timing. The "knower" is willing to wait until the last minute for his or her intentions to manifest. The "novice" is not.

MY INTENTION FOR TODAY IS:

· · · · · · · · · · · · · · · · · ·

*I Intend that I am willing to wait as
long as it takes for my intentions to manifest.*

TOLERANCE

· · · · · · · · · · · · · · · ·

*It's not about what happens to you. It's about
what you do with what happens to you.*

It's been our habit to try and make sense of everything that happens in our lives. We often take our experiences personally, thinking that things are happening to us, and we constantly analyze so that our uncomfortable situations won't repeat themselves.

What we don't realize is that we don't need to understand everything. In fact, if were always seeking to gain some understanding about what is happening to us, we run the risk of missing the beauty that's in the message we were meant to receive from our experiences.

Mariel had started the giant wok heating on the woodstove, and the smell of fresh, stir-fried vegetables floating through the air was making Johnny Waters more comfortable by the minute. He wasn't going to starve. Everything he had, except for what he could carry in his hands, was gone; and yet, he was happy. His job, his house, the car, the pension, all his money was gone; yet he was alive and well. Very well, in fact. He could see there was plenty to keep him and Helena busy and productive. It felt great to be part of a family unit again. They would be able to contribute. There were projects all around them: gardens to grow, newsletters to proofread, grandkids to raise. There was always something to do on a farm, and there was so much for them to learn. It was never too late to learn!

This new Intention Process fascinated him. He had already put it to the test and it worked like a charm. In fact, it had worked so well that he sat there chuckling to himself. Just before the Mercedes picked them up that morning, they had been sitting on their suitcases alongside Highway 161 between East Saint Louis and Belleville. Helena had reminded him of Sally's story about the art of hitchhiking. She said that it was a lot easier to spend a couple of minutes intending to get a safe, comfortable ride, than it was to stand out there in the hot sun all day with your thumb stuck out in the breeze.

MY INTENTION FOR TODAY IS:

*I Intend that I am seeing the benefit
in everything that happens to me.*

DISCERNING

*Our challenge is not to learn to manifest—for we are
all masters of the art— but instead to have a greater
discernment over that which we are already manifesting.*

As we said in the beginning, we're moving into a time when
all manifestations will become instantaneous; when we
will have a thought and it will be there. If you look back
over the last twenty to thirty years, you can see that this
is so. It wasn't long ago that you could make an intention to fulfill a desire and it seemed to take weeks or even
months to manifest. Nowadays, however, you can make
an intention and step around the next corner and practically trip over your manifestation. Everything is speeded up.
Our evolution and all of the powers that accompany it are
accelerating at a pace that calls forth the best within us just
to keep up. The next few years will be a training ground for

us to see if we can be responsible to that which serves us. Will we create a life of abundance and joy or something else?

The times we live in could be likened to the baking of a cake. First, you break the eggs—that's a violent act right there. Then, you take a bunch of different ingredients and you dump them all together in a bowl, and you whip the heck out of them. And while you're whipping, when you look at the gooey mess that's in front of you, it's hard to imagine that anything good could ever come out of it. But after you pour it in a pan and add the heat and time in the oven, out comes a beautiful, delicious cake for you to enjoy.

It's the same with what we're going through in these times of great change. Almost everywhere you look, people are stressed. Our lives are filled with fear, suffering, scarcity, and deception, and, from the looks of it, you would hardly imagine that anything good could ever come out of the mess we're in. But it can. Indeed, a wondrous new paradise on Earth is in the making, and it is up to us to bring it into manifestation.

All great manifesters know that discernment comes with the territory. In a dualistic world such as ours, when we make an intention to fulfill a desire, its opposite always surfaces to test us. To pass the tests, three steps are required. First, we must focus on the original intention; that is to say, we need to be impeccable and of pure intent. Second, we must trust and have faith in ourselves. And third, we need to realize that we are cocreators. Our individual power is increased as we call upon a higher power to work with us. With this in mind, it follows that for us to manifest our desires and intentions instantaneously, we would be well served to call upon the highest power available. We can invoke this entity by whatever name we prefer: the essence of the Universe—the Highest Good—God.

Our power seeks us out now, yet it is we who will decide what to do with it. Can we be responsible to our highest and best interests? Our greatest tests lie in our ability to discern and remain focused on the positive. It's evident to those whose consciousness is awakening at this time that our experiences are flowing outward from our thoughts in each and every moment. Our challenge is not to learn to manifest—for we're all masters of the art—but to have a greater discernment over that which we are already manifesting. Indeed, we can create anything we choose. All experiences are equally available to us.

MY INTENTION FOR TODAY IS:

*I Intend that I am being
even more vigilant of my thoughts now.*

THE IDEAL DEAL

· ·

Instead of seeing anything as a problem,
see everything as an opportunity.

The work we do here at the Intenders is a labor of love. We get a lot of calls from people asking us "How do we fix this?" or "What can we do about that?" The subject matter changes constantly; however, it usually gravitates around health, money, relationships, keeping what we have, or getting rid of something we have that we don't want anymore.

What we've found is that it doesn't really matter what the subject is, our responses, in one way or another, are typically the same. "What is your ideal situation?" we'll ask. Or, "If this all turned out exactly the way you'd like, what would the end result look like to you?"

And then, when our callers begin to get clear about their ideal outcomes, we tell them to make an intention around it and hold their attention on that ideal until it manifests right in front of them.

In a nutshell, that is the key to manifesting. Our thoughts are always working their way out into the world around us. It doesn't matter whether our ideal is living in perfect health, having a new washing machine, or creating an entirely new, more comfortable lifestyle for ourselves. The way to get there is by intending and envisioning our ideal.

There is no reason, whatsoever, why every human being who walks this Earth couldn't be given everything that he or she needs. Scarcity, in all of its insidious forms, can be tucked neatly away into our past and replaced by abundance beyond measure. Oppression can give way to a life of total freedom, such as we have never before experienced. And fear can now be seen for what it truly is—a cry in the dark for attention, a call for the gift of comfort and peace.

As that loving attention is freely given without reservation, a light so bright will shine forth on everyone and everything. The streets will be filled with people smiling at each other, wanting one and all to experience the joy that comes when we live our lives to the fullest. Everywhere you look there will be peace. We are cleansed of all impurity by the Living Universe as It surrounds us and bathes us in the Highest Light imaginable. Once again we are as innocent as young babes, yet divinely empowered, and thrilled at the wonders that lie before us.

The scene above is just one of my ideals. You can take out a piece of paper and begin to describe yours now and know that, in the describing, you are taking your first step toward bringing them to life.

chapter three

THE CODE

INSIDE THE CODE

*The gift in the message is much more important
than the Being. The Being is only the message bringer.*

I WRITE THIS, NOT AS ONE WHO IS AN ADVANCED
spiritual being or sage, but as someone who is just like you,
going through the same trials and tribulations that life on
Earth in the beginning of the new millennium presents to all
of us. In truth, I am but a scribe who has been fortunate to
come across the Ten Intents of The Code and who has had an
opportunity to begin to integrate these principles into my own
life. I do not claim to have mastered them yet; however, I can
tell you that they have made a tremendous difference in the
way I deal with the world I live in.

For instance, in accordance with the First Intent—*Support
Life*—I can no longer bring myself to take part in any conver-

sation or activity that calls for violence as a viable solution to anybody's problems. In the past, I may have gotten fired up about one us-versus-them drama or another, but these never seemed to do anyone any good. Now, instead, I see the wisdom in taking a stand on behalf of all life, and I will not lend my energy to supporting any institution that calls me to harm another. By integrating this Intent into my life, I find that I am not as popular as I used to be in some crowds, but something has shifted within me. I can live with myself easier. I like myself better. My conscience is awakening.

Many things like this have happened to me since I learned The Code. In fact, the writing of two books about it has been a magical process in itself. Just as soon as each Intent was fleshed out on paper, it also started expressing itself in real life as an experience that moved me forward. As an example, after I put the finishing touches on the Sixth Intent, I walked outside to take a break (I was caretaking a place in the Sierras, near Kings Canyon/Sequoia National Park at the time), and not one but three eagles circled high overhead. I have never seen anything like it before or since. It let me know that I was doing the right thing; that I was doing what I came here to Earth to do. In the language of the Sixth Intent, it showed me I was Synchronized.

The Code is a very timely gift for those who are drawn to

it. Amidst an ever-changing world that, for many, is becoming more stormy and uncomfortable by the day, it offers a new set of guidelines that will help us navigate through the choppy waters. These guidelines are designed to help us personally and, at the same time, to help our world. We are not called upon to "drop out," nor do we have to patch anything up. Instead, when we align with The Code, we allow that which is collapsing to go away of its own accord, while we concentrate our energies on creating something entirely new.

From my own experiences, I can tell you that "something entirely new" is very expansive, very promising. It includes having a better world here on Earth to live in, as well as opening up to a whole host of other realms that are accessible to us from the inside.

MY INTENTION FOR TODAY IS:

I Intend that I am saying The Code once a day
and seeing what happens as a result.

THE FIRST INTENT ~ SUPPORT LIFE

I refrain from opposing or harming anyone.
I allow others to have their own experiences.
I see life in all things and honor it
as if it were my own. I support life.

These teachings are meant to reveal the true nature, the true power of your thoughts to you. Each thought you entertain either takes you closer to your joy or farther from it; and it is for you to discern, in each moment, which of your thoughts are serving you, and which of your thoughts are not serving you.

Since you are becoming that which you hold your attention upon, you would be wise to support life in all that you think and all that you say. Up until now, much has been hidden from mankind concerning the dynamics of your thoughts, and you have not been properly taught how to think. Now, however, these teachings are being made available to all so that you can sharpen your thinking processes and create better lives for yourselves.

As you truly look to support life, you will soon see that one of the most detrimental things you can do is to oppose someone else. When you oppose anyone, you invite your worst fears to come alive. By taking a defensive stance against anything or anyone, you are actually creating or setting the scene for you to be attacked. It works this way: your thoughts are always creating your future. When you are opposing others, it is because you are picturing someone else doing something bad to you. This is a thought, and, like all thoughts, it is working its way into the stream of your daily experience. Whether the person you are thinking about is a grouchy neighbor, a terrorist, a soldier, or an attacker of any kind doesn't matter. What matters is that you understand that your thought of being attacked is going to manifest as quickly as any other thought. You must learn that it is you who ultimately makes the choices about which thoughts to place your attention on. It is you who invites goodness or chaos into your experience. It is you who is responsible for your creation.

One of the great lessons of life is that you attract to yourself, and must live out in your everyday experience, that which you oppose. You must learn to allow others to go through life without your interference, and know that your unwanted experiences will cease only when you have finally relinquished your tendency to resist them. Your opposition to anything, be it a person or an institution, always makes things worse.

> **MY INTENTION FOR TODAY IS:**
> . . . .
> *I Intend I always remember that harming*
> *another will never give me the results I desire.*

THE SECOND INTENT ~ SEEK TRUTH
. . . .

I follow my inner compass and discard any beliefs
that are no longer serving me.
I go to the source. I seek truth.

Looking back over the course of my life, I've always been a seeker of truth. It's been in my bones since I was a little boy, and I never felt comfortable in a situation where I felt deceived or confined by an illusion. As a result, I lived for twenty-eight years as a hermit back in the hills of the Big Island of Hawaii in order to free myself from the deceptions and illusions so prevalent in today's culture.

During those years I spent much of my time with a teacher named B. J. who was a strong, lanky fellow looking curiously like some of the pictures I'd seen of St. Germain. When I met him, he said that he'd been an instructor with a present-day, quasi-mystery school, which operated out of the San Francisco

Bay Area during the 1960s and early '70s called the Morehouse. The primary draw to the Morehouse, he explained, was to help people get more of whatever it was that they wanted. Well, needless to say, that idea appealed to me.

One day while we were taking a break from pruning the avocado trees, B. J. said if I wanted to disentangle myself from the mainstream matrix, I could begin by seeking a higher truth, a truth which he said could be accessed by walking one of three paths: 1) the path of imitation; 2) the path of meditation; and/or 3) the path of experience.

The first path, which he said was the easiest, required us to find someone else who is an example of all that we wanted to be and imitate them. He said that many of our wise elders and teachers from the past, including Jesus, Mother Mary, Buddha, and White Buffalo Calf Woman fit into this category. He also recommended that I keep a copy of the I Ching handy. He said it was the oldest book on the planet, and that whenever I found myself in need of help, it would guide me to the highest truth. (I immediately went out and bought a copy of Carol Anthony's I Ching, and, to this day, I carry it with me wherever I go.)

The second path, according to B. J., is the path of meditation, and its promise is that we can go into the stillness of our mind and, there, discover the truth about whatever we want to know. This path, which he called the noblest, may take some practice, but it allows us to view our surroundings and circumstances from a calmer, more detached point of view. It reveals a bigger picture to us. All we have to do in order to avail ourselves of its magic is pose a question to ourselves, quiet the activity of our mind for a few minutes, and then wait in stillness and be open to receive an answer. The better we get at stilling the clamor of our extraneous thoughts, the quicker, he said, our answers will come to us.

The third path, which is the one taken by most people, nowadays, is the path of experience. He called it the bitterest, and said that life itself will dish out the exact experiences we need to enable us to find the truth. He explained that, at first, his mentors at the Morehouse felt that this path was much too difficult for us, and they recommended that we concentrate our energies on either one of the two easier paths. But then, after carefully observing those of us who had the strength to endure the path of experience, his mentors came to the conclusion that it's how we react to our experiences that matters. They discovered that when we approach our tests with an optimistic attitude, and are completely gentle and honest with ourselves, we place ourselves in the best possible position for gaining a true understanding of our Earthly illusions. They did issue a word of caution, however: they said that it may be a little disconcerting for some of us when we discover the degree to which we've allowed ourselves to become immersed in our illusions, and that it's important for us to remember that there's nothing wrong with buying into an illusion, just as long as when we become conscious of it, we retain our freedom of choice. He said that some illusions can be fun; it's when our illusions stop working for us that we need to let them go, or learn how to stay more balanced while we're still in the midst of them.

As we sat under the guava trees, smoking and swatting mosquitoes, I was totally enthralled by what he was saying. In fact, I couldn't remember anyone having ever talked to me like this before. Our conversation had risen above the everyday mundane level, and, to me, it felt like I was being nourished. It felt like somebody cared.

MY INTENTION FOR TODAY IS:

*I Intend that I remember
that I am strengthened by my adversity.*

THE THIRD INTENT ~
SET YOUR COURSE

I begin the creative process. I give direction to my life.
I set my course.

After watching thousands of people make and manifest their intentions over the years, we began to notice a common thread. We saw that those who started out their day by setting their intentions had an entirely different experience than those who didn't. Their lives had a direction to them. Things came easier for them. They struggled less and had more moments of pure joy because that's how you feel when your desires are being fulfilled. Here is a passage from my novel, *The Reunion: A Parable for Peace*, which brings this idea to light.

"So far, your journey has shown you that all things are alive. The wind, the animals, the bodies of water, Great Nature Herself—all are Living Beings with whom you can communicate. What you have forgotten is that Intent is a Living Being, as well. It waits, like an old friend, for you to call upon it. When you reestablish your friendship with Intent and set your course in life, your willpower will return. From then on, you will no longer need to rely upon other men, 'men who are violent by nature' to lead you. You will be your own leader."

Suddenly, a new strength came into my body. Something in my solar plexus relaxed. Then it felt like a fire began to smolder inside my belly. I knew, in that moment, that I could overcome anything.

"You must learn to use your power wisely, my brother, so that you can deliver The Code to your people," he said. "Your world has seen enough of violence. It needs someone who is firmly lined up with Great Oneness; someone who can set a course for others to follow."

Sitting Bull's words resonated deep within me, striking a chord I yearned to hear, but had almost forgotten about.

As if knowing my thoughts, he continued, "Perhaps if I tell you a story, it will help you set your course in life and walk the path you chose for yourself long ago," he said. "It was in the year 1876 and my people, the Lakota Sioux, were engaged in a fierce battle with the blue-coated soldiers along the Yellowstone River. Crazy Horse and I were leading our people, but he was too young and excited by the fighting to notice that we were losing far too many of our strongest braves, and it was time to retreat.

"I went to his side and pointed this out to him, but he was wanting to continue the fight. He rallied the remaining young warriors, and, against my insistence, he was readying to attack again. I had to do something to stop it.

"And so, while Crazy Horse and his men were preparing to charge, I walked slowly into the center of the battlefield, sat down cross-legged, lit my sacred pipe, and called upon my good friend, Intent. I began my offering by giving great thanks for Intent being with me, and I asked him to protect me while I prayed to Great Oneness for guidance.

"For over a quarter of an hour, the soldiers fired upon me. Bullets plowed up the ground all around my body, but none touched me. You see, my brother, Intent and I were old friends, and I knew I could count on him.

"When I saw that Crazy Horse and the young braves had finally come to their senses, I slowly put my pipe away and walked back to my horse. My people followed me that day because they saw the power of my connection with Intent."

He was still for a long time, and then said, "This is the Third Intent, my brother. You are to know that you can do anything when you have Set Your Course in life. You and all of your people are powerful beyond measure. You can create anything you choose. Your heart can be at peace, just as your world can be at peace. But first you must say goodbye to your apathy and begin to reacquaint yourself with your old friend, Intent.

MY INTENTION FOR TODAY IS:

I Intend that I am saying my gratitudes and intentions every day.

THE FOURTH INTENT ~ SIMPLIFY

* *

I let go so there is room for something better to come in.
I intend that I am guided, guarded, protected,
and lined up with the Highest Good at all times.
I trust and remain open to receive from both
expected and unexpected sources. I simplify.

As the Intenders began to grow, we talked a lot about trust. We all agreed that there is no issue more important in these transitional times than the issue of trust, and that each of us, in our own mysterious way, was faced with the decision whether or not to trust that our thoughts would, in fact, manifest as we intended them. We also had to decide whether to believe that a higher power was working behind the scenes of our lives. And each was confronted with choosing, at one time or another, whether to let go of whatever we're attached to, lest we remain stagnant and stuck in the mud of our old ways.

There is a short story Lee Ching told us which helped to bring the principle of simplifying our lives into focus. He said that if we're going to cross over a small stream and see what adventures await us on the other side, eventually we'd have to leave the side we're standing on and step across the water. According to him, most people are living like they have a foot on each side of the stream, and they're straddling it, while the water level is rising. If they don't make a move pretty soon, they're going to get wet.

This little analogy works on many levels. It relates to cleaning our homes insofar as if we don't let go of some of the old stuff that's been lying around for years, we may never have room for any new stuff to come in. Likewise, it can also pertain to ideas we're carrying around with us. As we move closer to the cultural transition that looms on the horizon, we're beginning to discover that many of our beliefs and ideas aren't serving us anymore. They're outdated or barely working, and we really can't count on them like we used to. Most of the information we're fed by the media fits into this category. An example, although it may not always be stated outright, is that being at war will make things better. This archaic idea no longer works for us, and it really never did. All caring, thinking people know that we simply cannot achieve peace as long as we support war, and yet, war is still the cornerstone upon which the foundation of our entire civilization is built. If, however, we truly want peace—if we intend that we have true and lasting peace—we must let go of our tendency to make war and replace it with a more positive approach of resolving our differences. We must let it go so that something new and better can come in.

> **MY INTENTION FOR TODAY IS:**
>
> *I Intend that I am guided, guarded, protected, and lined up with the Highest Good at all times.*

THE FIFTH INTENT ~ STAY POSITIVE

*I see good, say good, and do good. I accept the gifts
from all of my experiences.
I am living in grace and gratitude. I stay positive.*

It is within each of us to create our ideal by starting from where we are in this moment and expressing our gratitude for all things. We can change our thoughts, and change our lives, and change our world by becoming perpetual optimists and lifting our Spirits to the heights. This additional passage from *The Reunion* reveals more about the Fifth Intent.

"What agreements have you and I made?" I asked, after awhile. "I really don't remember them."

When he turned to face me, I felt like he was looking right through me. "Long ago, we made a pact, you and I, to come together so that I could assist you in your time of reawakening. Your path led you to Earth at this place and time where you fell asleep to the true knowledge of who you are and what you came here to do. Once, we walked by the northern seashore as brothers, and it was there you asked me to meet you here on this mountain to deliver you a message—a particular Intent of The Code."

"And what is the message, Chief Seattle?"

"I am to remind you to Stay Positive, my brother."

"Stay Positive?" I repeated.

"Yes, Robert, just as you did when you faced into that rogue storm moments ago. You stayed positive when you could have just as easily cursed Great Oneness, given up, and lain your body down to die. Instead, something deep within you allowed you to handle the crisis without complaint or reverting back to your old negative ways of thinking. You stayed positive and laughed, and in doing so, you created a way out for yourself."

"Wait a minute," I said. "Are you telling me that I had something to do with making it out of that storm alive? That doesn't make any sense. I was totally at the mercy of it all!"

"But here you are now. Alive and well. How do you explain that?"

"I don't know. Luck, I guess."

He laughed so loud it echoed throughout the entire grotto. It sounded like we were surrounded by a hundred Indians. I couldn't help but laugh some more myself.

"You did it, Robert," he said, after we quieted down. "This much I know. It wasn't luck that saved you, it was the Fifth Intent."

"The Fifth Intent?"

"Yes, my brother. Even if you don't know it, you tapped into the Fifth Intent. You chose to Stay Positive while everything around you was falling apart."

"I did?"

"Yes," he answered. "Unlike many who would have allowed their doubts and negative thoughts to take over and ruin their lives, you held steadfast to a positive outcome and trusted that you would be okay."

Chief Seattle was reinforcing what Grandmother had told me. It occurred to me that they were talking about the same thing, but coming at it from different angles so I would be sure to get the point.

"You see, Robert," he continued, "everything in your world exists because someone thought of it first. Your thoughts are immeasurably more powerful than you give them credit for. The Fifth Intent has been hidden from you so that others could keep you under their thumbs. But now, it is time for your people to fly free like the eagles, and it is for you to play a part in this by teaching them how to Stay Positive."

"And just how do I do that?" As with the other Intents, I was confused at first.

"By telling them what happened to you out there in the storm. You see, my brother, as they begin to view their challenges as gifts instead, they will eventually come to realize that it's wise for them to remain positive, even when they're in the middle of a crisis."

"I don't think most people are ready to hear that yet, Chief," I said.

"The biggest barrier you'll run into, Robert, is that many of your people have gotten into the habit of negative thinking. They have yet to realize that when they think negative, unserving, or harmful thoughts, that those thoughts create negative or harmful events. On the other hand, if they'd begin to put more of their attention on positive thoughts, thoughts of goodness and gratitude, then their lives—and their world— will change for the better."

> **MY INTENTION FOR TODAY IS:**
> . . . .
> *I Intend that I am seeing myself, my friends, and my world in the highest light imaginable.*

THE SIXTH INTENT ~ SYNCHRONIZE

After intending and surrendering, I take action
by following the opportunities that are presented to me.
I am in the flow where great mystery and miracles abide,
fulfilling my desires, and doing what I came here to do.
I synchronize.

We've found that the recipe for successful creativity calls upon us to make use of three ingredients: intent, feeling, and action. The first ingredient, intent, is applied to define a desired outcome or goal. Our experience has taught us that when we make an intention, it's wise to be exact about what we desire to manifest, but to leave the specifics undefined when it comes to how or when our intentions will come to us. By following this guideline and invoking the Highest Good, we allow the Universe to utilize any one of an infinite variety of ways to bring our intention into manifestation. Intenders who cling to a single or specific route in seeking to create their abundance limit the magical workings of the Universe considerably.

The second ingredient, feeling, comes into the picture in order to provide the energy needed to make our intention develop from a thought into an etheric reality that is poised and ready to blossom into the world around us. In observing many of our Mighty Manifesters over the years, we've come to understand that those who are able to conjure up the feeling they'll be experiencing after their goal has been reached (even though it may not have actually manifested in physical reality yet), achieve vastly better results than those who are not in touch with the power of their feelings. Said another way, if a person can maintain the feeling of gratitude in advance of the actual manifestation of their intentions, they will increase their rate of success immensely.

As our intentions begin to precipitate down from the invisible into physical manifestation, we need to be ready to apply the third ingredient: action. Before taking action, however, there has to be a waiting period or pause which typically lasts a few days (although the amount of time may vary depending upon the proficiency of the manifester and whether the Highest Good is being served or not). This is when we let go of all attachments and concerns about our creative endeavors and retreat into a state of divine nonchalance. Taking this conscious pause allows the Universe to work at its own pace in arranging things. Then, after the waiting period is over and our intention is ready to come forth, we'll notice that a series of synchronistic "coincidences" begins to appear in our lives. We will have stepped into a magical flow that is characterized by a sequence of events occurring around us that is moving us toward our desired outcome. When this flow of seemingly magical "coincidences" reveals itself, it's up to us to take the appropriate action, which each synchronistic event calls for until our final goal is reached.

If, for instance, we've intended to meet our soul mate, and an attractive new person enters our life, then we would pursue that opportunity to find out if this is the love of our life, or if it is simply a contact with someone who has something else to offer us as we continue moving toward our desired relationship.

If we think we've met a potential soul mate, then we would take action to get to know this person better so we can see where the relationship leads. They may be the one who we've been longing for, or perhaps they may be someone who will introduce us to our soul mate. In either case, as opportunities like this present themselves, it's up to us to provide the appropriate action until our intention is materialized. The idea is to keep moving forward. Sometimes all we'll have to do is hold out our hand or answer the phone, but, most often, our goals are realized by following a synchronistic chain of events and opportunities, each of which leads us ever closer to "the grand finale," which is the manifestation of our original intention.

If you're choosing to walk the path of empowerment, you'll need to get good at making your intentions, letting them go, and then taking action when opportunities present themselves. Taking action is where synchronicity comes in. If it's for your Highest Good, usually within a few days after you've surrendered your intentions up to the Universe, a series of almost surprising events will reveal themselves to you, and it is for you to move forward from one to the next until you reach your final goal. Suddenly, you'll notice that you're in a serendipitous flow where all good things are coming to you and that everything you need is magically there for you when you need it. From then on, all you have to do is stay alert to that which is in front of you until, one day, when Great Mystery opens her arms wide in the form of a feeling you've rarely experienced and probably forgotten about. Your innocence will return, and life—the life you were truly meant to live—becomes an adventure once again.

MY INTENTION FOR TODAY IS:

I Intend that whatever needs to be known
is revealed to me in the moment I need
to know it, or sooner.

THE SEVENTH INTENT ~ SERVE OTHERS

*I practice love in action. I always have enough
to spare and enough to share.
I am available to help those who need it.
I serve others.*

As we shift into the new paradigm and move away from an attitude of service-to-self to one of service-to-others, we'll each, in our own way, come to a point when we realize that service to others is service to oneself. This usually happens when we get a glimpse of what our world would be like if everyone was serving everyone else. It's easy to see that we would all be much happier, be more abundant, and feel less fearful if we were all serving each other. War, poverty, unrest, starvation, and the like wouldn't exist because we wouldn't allow our brothers and sisters to suffer like we do nowadays. We'd be helping them instead.

"When I first decided to serve others, I didn't realize that it also included forgiving them. I thought I would help them out by cleaning or running errands or doing whatever they wanted, but what I came to understand was that I could help them in other ways as well.

The instance that brought all of this home to me was when I made an intention to help my aging mother. In 1998, I gave up my own apartment, moved in with my mom, and began to prepare her food, bathe her, and do all of the things necessary to make her last days as comfortable as possible. Up until then, I really hadn't made much of an effort to get close to her. She lived three states away, and we really didn't get along all that well anyway. In truth, there were long periods of time when we never spoke at all because I was still carrying a lot of anger toward her for things she'd done to me as a child. Mainly, I never understood how she could just stand by and let my father abuse me like he did.

But in the last few weeks of her life, as she lay in her deathbed with me sitting in the chair beside her, we began to talk about some of the things that we might not have otherwise spoken about. One particular evening after we finished eating and our barriers were lower than usual, I asked her why she let my dad beat me without ever coming to my rescue. Her answer showed me a side of her I never knew existed.

She explained that she was just as afraid of him as I was, that he beat her and threatened her too, and that he was always very careful not to let anyone else know about it. She was so sorry, she said, but at the time she was totally incapable of giving me the love I needed because she was in fear for her own safety.

She started to cry when she told me the details. I felt such compassion for her, laying there in her bed like that, waiting to die any day. But, most of all, I felt sorry because we'd never talked like this before. When her tears stopped, and as I was wiping them from her cheeks, she touched my arm with her frail hand and asked me to forgive her for not being a good mother. She said she really loved me, both then and now, and that it would mean a lot to her if I could find forgiveness in my heart for her.

I didn't move except to brush away the tears from my own eyes. Suddenly, a very emotional experience when I was a teenager came to mind. My mother was in a bad mood and had punished me for something I was innocent of. It was in that moment that I had decided, resolutely, to put her out of my life. Now, however, as I recalled that highly charged event, I was able to see the unhappiness in her face that I didn't see before. I never knew she was that unhappy.

As my vision of the past receded, she looked up at me from her bed, our eyes met, and I told her that I forgave her, not just for that instance, but for everything uncaring she'd ever done to me. Then I leaned down to hug her, and as I did, it felt like a great weight was lifted from my chest. We both wept some more that night, and, after that, something shifted in me...and in her. From then on, until the time she passed away, she was much calmer and at peace. The way I see it, our forgiveness healed us both."

—ALAN MATOUSEK

MY INTENTION FOR TODAY IS:

I Intend that I'm available to help others and that I always have enough to spare and enough to share.

THE EIGHTH INTENT ~
SHINE YOUR LIGHT

I am a magnificent Being, awakening to my highest potential. I express myself with joy, smiling easily and laughing often. I shine my light.

Working directly with the light is our next step. It doesn't cost us anything to see ourselves happier, more abundant, or full of joy. No one sends us a bill when we see our body in its ideal state of health. We don't need anyone's permission, and we don't have to be in a special place. Nor do we require the use of any fancy devices or tools. In fact, we don't need anything other than our imagination and the light itself, and it's always there, just waiting for us to do with as we please. It doesn't take long working with the light until we begin to shine brighter than ever. A scene from *The Reunion* shows the value of working with the light.

I don't know how long I slept, but when I awoke, a radiantly beautiful woman stood before me. She was dressed in a white-fringed, buckskin dress, intricately beaded with ancient Native American symbols. An eagle feather was tied to her single black braid, and beside her stood a young, pure white buffalo, grazing quietly. I knew from the stories I'd read years ago that she was White Buffalo Calf Woman.

"You're real!" I blurted out.

"I'm as real as you are," she answered, smiling at me.

"But I thought you were a myth or a fairy tale."

She laughed out loud. "Much is not as it appears to be."

I thought about that and nodded.

She looked at me thoughtfully, her eyes showing a genuine compassion. "You are very close to stepping further into the world of Spirit," she said. "In the world of Spirit, all is known. No secrets exist, and no one can hide. Those who live in Spirit see all that goes on in the world of Matter. But those in the world of Matter do not see into the world of Spirit, unless they learn to shine their light."

"And how do I learn to shine my light?" I asked.

"By doing just what you are doing, Robert. By overcoming your fears. By taking responsibility for your own actions and stepping bravely into the unknown. By asking for guidance, like you did in your intentions this morning."

I didn't say anything. As far as I was concerned, there were still a lot of things that I was afraid of.

"I will give you an example," she said. "When you came upon this magical living stream, you didn't hesitate to drink all you wanted. You trusted in your intuition that the water was good for you, and you weren't frightened to touch it."

"That's true."

* * *

"Many people in your world would not have done what you did. They would think the water was poisonous, and they would shy away from it. Their beliefs would have kept them from experiencing the special revitalizing qualities that this water passes on to those who drink of it." She reached down and ran her hand, ever so slowly, through the water. From where I sat, it looked like a thousand diamonds glistening as the water trickled through her fingers.

"It is the same with many things in your world. Your people are frightened of things that, in reality, are very beneficial for them."

"What things?" I asked.

"You labor under two great limitations, Robert. These limitations pervade your world and keep you from experiencing your birthright. The first limitation is that there are no worlds other than the one in which you are living. It amazes those in my world how this idea can continue to exist, especially in light of all of the new information, which is being made available to you. Where do you think your dreams are coming from? Where do your thoughts, your feelings, or your creative inspirations come from? There is so much more that awaits your people, and yet they cannot access it as long as they believe it doesn't exist."

"Our limiting beliefs create our limited reality?" I stated, rhetorically.

"That's the way it works, Robert. If, on the other hand, your people would seek, in earnest, to step into the world of Spirit, then ancient doors would open, and old friends would bid them to enter."

MY INTENTION FOR TODAY IS:

I Intend that I take some time every day to see myself in my highest light.

THE NINTH INTENT ~ SHARE YOUR VISION

I create my ideal world by envisioning it and telling others about it. I share my vision.

If we truly desire to create a better world for ourselves, we would need to do something different than what we've been doing. We'd need to think different thoughts and talk about different things. At present, our thoughts and words are dominated by ideas that keep us separated from one another, beliefs that we are limited, and outcomes that have little or no value to us personally, or to humanity at large. It's as if we have all the tools we need to create a paradise on Earth, and yet, these tools sit idle while we remain confused about what we really came here to do.

Fortunately, as we've seen from the stories in this book, many of us are breaking free from our urge to conform to the old ways of doing things, and we are bringing others of like-mind along with us. Soon, enough of us will be thinking and talking about that which truly serves us and we will create a better world.

The next time you find yourself grumbling about the way things are in the world, and you feel powerless to change any of it, take out a notebook and start writing about what your ideal world would look like to you. Describe, in detail, anything that comes to mind. You might choose to depict your ideal environment, the way you'd like people to act toward you, your perfect neighborhood, your ideal personal life, etc. Write down the final outcome, not the steps it takes to get there. Leave those up to God.

Write as much as you feel like writing and then, when you've finished, take a mental snapshot of the visions you've written about and imprint each one indelibly in your mind.

And the next time you're in the company of friends who are expressing their concern for the way things are going lately, instead of commiserating and feeling disempowered, share your mental snapshots with them. Do just as you'd do if you'd brought along your picture album from last summer's vacation. Point out all the little things they might miss, and, above all, tell them that their thoughts have the power to create a better world, and let them know that when they're envisioning their ideal world and sharing it with others, they are bringing it to life.

MY INTENTION FOR TODAY IS:

I Intend that I am sharing my visions of my ideal world and knowing that, in the sharing, I am consciously contributing to the creation of them.

CREATING YOUR NEW WORLD

To participate on another level, you need not know how. Just know that you want to.

Over the last three years, many people have shared their visions with us and the overall feeling we get from rereading these inspiring visions is that the people who told them to us had awakened from their indifference and were now more enlivened and empowered to make their world a better place in which to live. What excited us most was that these people frequently mentioned that they felt so empowered by what they were doing that they couldn't wait to get together with their friends and ask them the question: *If you were already living in your ideal world, when you look around yourself, what do you see?*

We have left a space at the end of this step for you to jot down some visions of your own. If you'd like, you can even share your visions with the world by publishing them to our website at www.visionalignmentproject.com.

Oh, and by the way, you needn't be concerned if the details of your visions are different than someone else's. It's the intent behind your vision that counts. Feel free to express yourself as you like, and know that when you set your intent for a better world, a better world will come to you.

Now it's time for you to create your own vision. But before you do, it might help to take a deep breath and imagine for a few moments that everything you see around you is made out of light, and that you can have a direct effect on your world by using your imagination. Now breathe deeper, and let go even more. Let go of any immediate cares for your survival needs;

let go and feel your true joy settle in as all of your Earthly cares and concerns disappear. This is where you find your safe haven. This is where you are free to create to your heart's content.

Now that you're relaxed, you can prepare to formulate your vision of a better world. Know that everything you need is here for you. All sounds are within you. All sights are within you. All thoughts and feelings are within you. All That Is is within you, and all you have to do is close your eyes and let God show you how beautiful your new world can be.

And, when you're ready, you can share your vision here:
I see a world where...

_____

_____

_____

_____

(If you would like to make a difference and know that you are consciously contributing to the creation of a better world for all of us to live in, you can go to the Vision Alignment Project at www.visionalignmentproject.com and align with our Visions. Perhaps you'll even share your own Vision with us there!)

THE TENTH INTENT ~ SYNERGIZE

. . . .

I see Humanity as One. I enjoy gathering
with lighthearted people regularly.
When we come together, we set the stage for
Great Oneness to reveal Itself.
We synergize.

Now that we've formulated our visions of a better world and expanded them by sharing them with others, it's time to bring them into physical manifestation. To do this, we must come together. We must begin to make good use of the gifts that community has to offer.

In the dozen years that I've been taking part in Intenders Circles across the country, I've seen a lot of amazing things happen within the dynamics of a group. I've seen people who were introverted and frightened open up; I've seen my friends totally and utterly fulfilled; I've seen strangers recognize each other as long-lost soul family; I've seen tears of joy flow and laughter abound. But there is one thing that happens in our Intenders Circles that, to me, is better than all the rest. It's what I call Synergy and, if we do things right, and set the stage properly, a very special feeling—a feeling of Oneness—will engulf the room and everyone in it. When this happens, it's as if we've completely let go of our connection to the cares and worries of the day and melted into something larger than ourselves. That's what Synergy is; it's what occurs when the whole becomes something greater than the sum of its individual parts. Put another way, it's when you put things together and "something extra" that you may not have expected takes place.

I have memories of a time, tens of thousands of years ago, when we were much more powerful than we are now. Groups of eight of us (or sometimes sixteen) would go into caves especially designed for their symmetry and we would sit in a perfect circle with giant crystals behind us which were connected to the crystalline benches we sat on. We agreed beforehand on a few specific objects that we intended to manifest, and then we would meditate and concentrate our imagination on those objects—and soon, sometimes instantaneously, they would materialize at a point in the exact center of the circle, floating in midair, right in front of us.

What we found in our Intenders Circles is that we can set the stage for an experience of Synergy to occur by following the Oneness Formula, which consists of six steps we go through after everyone has finished stating their gratitudes and intentions. They are: 1) sitting or standing together in a circle; 2) touching; 3) inviting; 4) turning; 5) toning; and 6) holding the silence. We've discovered that when we follow these steps, the electricity, the magic, the Oneness, the special feeling which brings us closer to God usually happens. We have taken the adage "Anywhere two or more are gathered in My Name (or for the Highest Good)," and put it to its best use. After all, isn't that what people are supposed to do when they gather together for spiritual purposes? Wouldn't it be wise for us to explore the highest of experiences available to us whenever we come together? These are some of the questions we sought to answer as we began to tap into the power of the Intenders Circle.

MY INTENTION FOR TODAY IS:

I Intend that I remember that in order to have peace, people must work together.

chapter four

UNIVERSAL TRUTHS

RELATING

That's why human beings are here—
to live their lives fully and freely.

IN TODAY'S TOPSY-TURVY WORLD, WE SEEM TO have set aside any guidelines for relating to one another. If we were to believe everything we see and hear in the media, it's all just fine and dandy for us to do anything we like to somebody else.

Certainly, our current world leaders set the worst of examples, advocating violence at every turn; while our true heroes—the ones who have the courage and integrity to stand up on behalf of life's virtues—go mostly unnoticed nowadays.

Fortunately, the media isn't the only source we have for guidance and information. We have our own inner guidance that will tell us how to relate to each other in all situations if we will only use it.

Back in the early '70s, my first teacher, B. J., passed an interesting idea along to me about how to behave toward one another. I'll pass it on to you now so you can try it on for size and see how it works for you. He said that one of the great rules of life is that you can give yourself all the pleasure you like, just as long as nobody else is getting pain because you're giving yourself pleasure.

MY INTENTION FOR TODAY IS:

I Intend that I am doing no harm.

MULTITASKING

*You deserve to have the kind of setting
which supports you.*

Our culture today requires many of us to do several jobs at the same time. In fact, multitasking has become the standard in our lives: we talk on the cell phone, while we work on an important memo for the office, while we add to the day's grocery list, while we stand in line at the restaurant, while we... We've become so accustomed to constantly stimulating ourselves that we're even apt to poke fun at those who do not share our penchant for multitasking. They're too slow, we say, or they're too inefficient. Thank God we don't have to work with them on a regular basis, or we'd end up in the loony bin!

The other side of the coin is more contemplative, more meditative, and those who prefer it live a somewhat calmer lifestyle. They know the wisdom in doing one thing at a time, and doing it well. They subscribe to the "quality is better than quantity" mindset, advocating that the world would be a better place for all of us if we'd just slow down and take a closer look at our immediate surroundings.

So, who is right? Both are.

And which way is best for us personally? That depends on our calling, or what we came here to do.

Clearly, some people need to accomplish great worldly things, and in order to do so they have to keep several irons in the fire at all times. Likewise, others came here to explore their inner environment, and all of the stimuli that come with multitasking act as a constant distraction to them. Their point of view suddenly becomes more valid when held up against the light of putting our attention to its highest and best use. For there is one thing that the contemplative person is able to do that the multitasker isn't: he or she can hold their attention on any one thing easier than someone who is overstimulated. They can look deeply into and discover the essence of things. Indeed, it is in the holding of our attention on any one thing that all things are revealed to us.

One day B. J. and I were pruning a stand of overgrown avocado trees on the lower section of the land in Kona. The job required us taking turns running a chain saw way up in the trees, keeping track of the cuts we were making, tying ropes, watching out for weak limbs, etc. We had to hold our attention on several things at the same time.

Sometime late in the morning we were both hot and sweaty, so we decided to take a break. As B. J. leaned back against the trunk of the tree we were working on, he started talking. "You know, Tony, most people can learn to juggle. With a little practice, the average person can easily keep three balls in the air at the same time. It's when they add the fourth ball that they get into trouble."

"Uhhuh," I said, wondering where he was going with this idea.

"Yeah," he said, "you see it all the time in people's lives. They'll be working to keep their job running smoothly, their family happy, and perhaps they'll have a hobby, like tennis or tinkering with a custom car in the garage. Most people can handle doing three things at the same time. It's when they add the fourth that things get weird. For instance, let's say that they've got the job, the family, and their spiritual development going along fine, and then they decide to take on another part-time job, for whatever reasons. That's when people's lives begin to fall apart."

"It's an interesting analogy," I commented.

"It's more than an analogy," he replied emphatically. "It's a very real phenomenon of human consciousness. People don't realize how they affect their lives and the lives of those around them when they take on new projects. Like I said, most people can easily juggle three balls; it's when they add the fourth one that *all* of the balls get dropped."

> ### MY INTENTION FOR TODAY IS:
>
> *I Intend that I am creating a living environment for myself where I am easily able to keep my attention focused on my priorities.*

A HIGHER POINT OF VIEW

Adversity strengthens us. Who could we learn more from than our own brothers and sisters?

It is time that we start looking at our lives from the level of the soul. At present, most people have bought into the limiting idea that this life is the only one there is, but nothing could be further from the truth. Indeed, as it has been said many times throughout these writings, we live countless lifetimes in countless realities, all for the purpose of expanding our creativity. Sometimes we even take on tasks that require us to learn lessons that are not always pleasant in the short run.

Our soul is an enthusiastic, adventurous vehicle, but our body tends toward complacency and becoming comfortable with routines. It seems that we need our apple cart upset every so often in order to break us out of our malaise. This is why we made agreements and arrangements with others, before we came into this lifetime, to help each other in case we started to get stuck here. We asked our soul family to show up at the right time to provide the perfect lesson that would get us moving forward again.

For those who don't see this wondrous play going on from a higher, soul level, it would appear as if the person who is creating all of our turmoil and adversity is a horrible bad guy. Those who are wedded to their Earthly identity tend to make judgments, play the blame game, and grumble incessantly about the harsh conditions imposed on them by someone else. However, in truth, our adversaries are just doing what we asked them to do long, long ago, in a place beyond this beautiful Earth. Here is an excerpt from *The Reunion: A Parable for Peace* that explains this further.

"You labor under two great limitations, Robert. These limitations pervade your world and keep you from experiencing your birthright. The first limitation is that there are no worlds other than the one in which you are living. It amazes those in my world how this idea can continue to exist, especially in light of all of the new information, which is being made available to you. Where do you think your dreams are coming from? Where do your thoughts, your feelings, or your creative inspirations come from? There is so much more that awaits your people, and yet they cannot access it as long as they believe it doesn't exist."

"Our limiting beliefs create our limited reality?" I stated, rhetorically.

"That's the way it works, Robert. If, on the other hand, your people would seek, in earnest, to step into the world of Spirit, then ancient doors would open, and old friends would bid them to enter."

MY INTENTION FOR TODAY IS:

I Intend that I am looking at life from my soul's point of view.

PROJECTS OR PROBLEMS

*Think if you could be doing what it is that makes you the most happy.
Then go and do it.*

The ancient Chinese *I Ching* tells us that it furthers one to have something to do. Likewise, the powerful Gurdjieff and Ouspensky teachings from the Caucasus of Russia talk about the great wisdom in having a project to keep our attention on. They say that we must put our creative abilities to work if we are going to raise our level of consciousness. Put in today's terms, we can see that it serves us to have a project to occupy our time, lest we begin to create problems for ourselves. In fact, there appears to be a direct correlation between the amount of idle time we have and the amount of dramas and problems in our lives. (Needless to say, the TV hasn't helped us in this regard either.)

Ultimately, it is a question of balance. We require a certain amount of downtime in order to digest our experiences and re-create ourselves. Conversely, if we spend too much of our time being idle, problems begin to arise for us. The trick is to find something you like to do, and do it; while, at the same time, you need to know how to take a break when you need it. Once you get good at recognizing the ebb and flow of this cycle, you'll be a lot happier than those who aren't aware of it.

MY INTENTION FOR TODAY IS:

I Intend that I am rising above life's challenges by becoming a more conscious creator.

LOOKING WITHIN

Your mind will run you around, lifetime after lifetime, until you still it.

The world we live in is but one among an infinite number of realms and realities that are available to us. Joys and wonders abound in places that only become known when we are able to stop the constant onslaught of our egos.

Indeed, when we take into consideration the vastness of All That Is, the part of us that is our persona, our ego, is very small, so small in fact as to be almost inconsequential in the great scheme of things. Of course, it would have us thinking otherwise. In seeking constant validation for its own existence, the ego has us telling ourselves that we know better than others, that we're smarter than most everyone else (even if our IQ hovers near dog-level), and that the world would be a marvelous place if others would just follow our lead. In short, our ego is lying to us every step of the way, and it is for us to find our way out of the maze of lies so our Spirit can shine forth.

That's what's important. Our Spirit calls out for release, for unbounded expression, for love and expansion. While, at the same time, our ego blocks the awakening of our Spirit with its constant distraction by mundane trivialities and survival issues which are, most often, unfounded. Isn't it time that we put the ego in its place? How about, for openers, if we give it the same consideration that we give our body every summer? How about we give it a two-week vacation so our Spirit can come out and party for a while?

The destiny of men and women on Earth today is not to be found chasing after the promise of the American Dream. Those of us who grew up in the baby boomer generation have seen the American Dream come and go. It has outlived its usefulness. There was a time when it was very attractive, but it has left many of us feeling empty. One day, we may have been at the top of the material world, enjoying all of its bounty; and, the next day, that bounty could become burdensome or nonexistent, leaving us to wonder why we spent so much time and energy pursuing it.

A common thread that runs through the minds of many of us is that there has to be more to life. There has to be something we can do, or someplace we can go, to achieve the lasting happiness that we instinctively know to be ours. Fortunately, there is a place we can go for fulfillment that offers us a vast range of wonderful experiences. This place lies within us— each and every one of us. As we close our eyes and be still for a few moments, sights, sounds, and feelings that were once hidden show themselves to us. We realize that we are more than our body. We are a Being who lives inside our physical body, and this Being continues to exist long after the physical body is gone.

As we practice looking within, we find that the Spiritual Being who lives inside us, is not encumbered by the man-made rules, contrived scenarios, and survival needs of the physical body. It is unlimited. It can take us to worlds we didn't previously know existed. Suddenly, we discover that the true destiny of man and woman is having free access to higher states of consciousness. We see that our future lies in other realms, other dimensions, other Universes. We feel like a seed which has remained dormant for a long time which has now popped its head above the soil, spread its new leaves out for all the world to see, and is reaching its young branches up to the sky.

> **MY INTENTION FOR TODAY IS:**
> . . . .
> *I Intend that I am taking some time today to look within.*

NO SECRETS
. . . .

Every one of us is seen and known for who we truly are.

One of the chief characteristics of the accelerated times we're living in is an enhancement of our perceptions. For some of us, our intuition is awakening, and we are now able to know things that we never knew before. Some people use muscle testing, dowsing rods, or pendulums, while others are simply finding themselves able to quiet their minds long enough for their Higher Self to come forth. When our Higher Self steps in we will have no need of books or channels or divination tools anymore. The answers to all of our questions will be made known from within. Such is the destiny for all who choose it.

Another kind of perceptual enhancement is the opening of our third eye. Lee Ching used to tell us to hold our attention a little above the place between our eyebrows and that after practicing this for a while in our meditations, we would be able to "see" into the essence of things. He told us that once our third eye opened we would be aware of things that are right in front of us, but which are currently invisible to us while we're in our present state of consciousness.

B. J. put it another way. He said that "the higher see the lower, but the lower don't see the higher." From his point of view, there were no secrets in our world. Each one of us carried our past and our probable futures with us, and anyone with their third eye open could see into the lives of others.

One cloudy afternoon I was walking up the trail to B. J.'s coffee shack after having gone into Kailua town to get some things for the farm. I was humming a popular America ballad from the early '70s that I was planning to learn to play on the guitar. As I dropped off some of the supplies and was getting ready to leave, B. J. picked up an old tattered piece of paper that was sitting on the counter beside his kitchen sink, and said, "Hey Tony. I ran across this the other day and was going to throw it away but thought you might be interested in it."

He handed it to me, and I opened it up. It was the sheet music to the song I was humming earlier.

> **MY INTENTION FOR TODAY IS:**
>
> *I Intend that my perceptions are becoming enhanced in perfect accordance and timing with that which is for my Highest Good.*

TRUE COMMUNICATION

You don't really have it unless you can give it away.

We have a stereotype of the Master Teachers as being calm, cool, and collected all the time, without a predilection for emotional behavior. Well, B. J. wasn't that way at all. In fact, he wouldn't hesitate to raise the intensity level in our conversations, and it wasn't until years later I realized that that was what he had to do simply to get my attention.

He used to say that communication is much more than talking. We can talk until we're blue in the face and never really communicate. Communication, he said, is the art of taking an idea or point of view that is in our head and doing whatever we have to do in order to get it into the other person's head. Unless that happens, he said, we were just talking, not communicating. And, in my case, if talking wasn't working, he would invariably devise some sort of challenge for me to go through so that I'd have to experience what he was talking about. In other words, he used every means available to get his messages across.

One day while we were building a large wooden rack to store our lumber and tools so the Kona rainforest wouldn't reclaim everything right away, B. J. was talking about the three stages we must go through if True Communication is to occur. The initial stage was called Agreement, and he said that we'd never get our ideas across to someone else if we didn't get into agreement with them first. His example was, "Oh, you're interested in Economics, well, so am I," and we would talk about Economics long enough for me to get comfortable with him and his points of view. According to him, sometimes getting into agreement took a long time and sometimes it happened right away; it all depended on the skill of the person who was committed to communicating their ideas. Likewise, it didn't matter what the subject matter was. It could be Economics or the Philadelphia Phillies. A Master, he said, was adept at discussing a wide variety of subjects, and it wasn't the subject at hand he cared so much about, but that he stayed in agreement at this stage of the relationship. I remember he used to say, "Tony, the symbols (or subjects) always change, but the functions remain the same."

After we were in agreement long enough for me to be at ease with him, he began to go into the second stage of true communication: Reality. Reality, he said, is exemplified by, "I like the Phillies and you like the Mets." Those are our realities, and it's okay if they differ from one another. At this stage, he asked my permission to go on because he didn't want to be manipulating me or doing anything I didn't want him to do. We had reached an understanding that it was okay to express our own ideas. In short, we had agreed to disagree. Later he told me that if we disagreed with someone too soon, they would be apt to tune us out, and our chances from then on of communicating with them got much slimmer. But if we stayed in agreement to the point where we could openly discuss our individual realities, then we could safely move on to the third stage, which he called True Communication, or the true taking of a thought or picture that's in our mind and transferring it into someone else's mind.

True Communication, as B. J. described it, is much trickier than most of us give it credit for. Patience, perseverance, and commitment are required, and it can take anywhere from a few minutes to a few years for us to successfully pass our ideas along to another person.

The truth be known, B. J. and I were together for over seventeen years, and when he disappeared, there were still a couple of his ideas that I still hadn't integrated yet. My guess is that he's in another reality somewhere, doing whatever is necessary to communicate his thoughts to me from there.

MY INTENTION FOR TODAY IS:

*I Intend that I am becoming adept
at communicating my ideas to others.*

RECEIVING YOUR OWN MESSAGES

Create with Love and your creation will Love you back.

I have a copyright on my work, but I can't say I'd enforce it if someone with good intent wanted to take a portion of it and use it. In fact, there is one piece of information that I've gleaned in the last few years that I would encourage my readers to copy down and use freely. My good friend, Debra Ward, who runs the Intenders Circle in Houston, calls it "The Intenders Prayer." It has to do with the instructions I give myself before sitting down and picking up a pencil or speaking to a group of people.

I've come to realize that there is an exactness, a clarity, that is required when we begin to make contact with helpers from other dimensions. Whether we know it or not, all of us are receiving messages from the invisible a good deal of the time. Entities from invisible worlds come and go from our bodies and we don't even realize that what we're saying may not be coming from us, but from a being who just popped into our body to pursue its own interests. We're a world full of people who have given free rein to the rest of the energies in the Universe, to use our bodies at their discretion. If you think about it, this would explain all of the mood swings, self-detrimental activities, and violent and nonproductive behavior you see all around and within you. We're simply letting some invisible beings use our bodies.

A good example of this can be found in the writings of most of our present day, best-selling authors. Stephen King, for instance, has surely tapped into an almost unlimited source of information (he says it's a cigar-chomping muse). But the fearful nature of his work suggests that it's doubtful if his muse is interested in creating a better world for us to live in.

Indeed, we can enhance our creativity and beneficent behavior by using this new knowledge wisely. We can invite beings that only stand for the Highest Good to use our bodies. We can issue clear instructions to those who would come in and borrow our voices or our writing hands.

I know that this will sound like an oversimplification to

many of you, but I suggest that it is entirely possible that the world we live in would make a monumental change for the better if we were to stop for a moment before we say or do anything that is of value to us and give ourselves brief instructions for what we desire to follow. My whole world began to change when I began to stop and take a minute or two to talk to the Universe each time the outcome of my actions was important to me (which became more and more frequent).

For me, taking that moment or two became the difference between caring and not caring. I began to see a noticeable difference in the quality of my work. And, at the same time, everything got a lot more enjoyable for me.

So, like I said, you can borrow my instructions if you like. Put them to the test. See what comes out. I intend for you all the best that life has to offer.

The instructions I use are:

1. *I ask that everything needing to be known is known here today.*

2. *I Intend that I am guided, guarded, and protected at all times.*

3. *I Intend that all of my words (or writings) are clear, precise, uplifting, helpful, and fun.*

4. *And I Intend that all of my words and thoughts and deeds serve the Highest and best Good of the Universe, myself, and everybody everywhere.*

So be it and so it is.

MY INTENTION FOR TODAY IS:

· ·

*I Intend that I am only attracting invisible
energies to me who stand
for the Highest Good.*

GRACE

· · · · · · · · · · · ·

*When man remembers his spiritual connection
to All That Is, he lives in a most joyous state,
wherever he is, whatever he is doing.*

The Intenders of the Highest Good would like to thank you
for joining us as we move toward our self-empowerment. It
is our firm intention to provide you with everything you
need to become a Mighty Manifester and create the life of
your choosing. At this point we'd like to present you with a
loving reminder. And we intend that you continue using these
reminders to become a powerful force dedicated to the Highest
Good of the Universe, yourself, and everyone you touch.

Remember...

That which is meant to be yours will come to you. Just as those of you who are aligned with the Highest Good will eventually experience your highest ideal, so shall your daily needs be met. You need never worry about your survival because there was a special mechanism put into place long ago, which regulates and guarantees that everything you need, will be there for you in the exact moment that you need it. Oftentimes it will not appear until the instant before it is needed, but you may be assured that while you are waiting you are being strengthened. As you learn to trust in this wondrous process, the obstacles and hardships of life fall by the wayside and are replaced by a serenity that knows no limit.

These times of great upheaval are truly gifts unto you. You are constantly surrounded by an environment that is conducive for bringing out your most fulfilling form of expression. Your ego, the part of you that is in service to yourself, is giving way to a much larger, grander you—the you that is in service to others. You are blossoming in all your glory, and it is this blossoming that you have always longed for. Be open, be available, and, in the meantime, be at peace. Your prayers and intentions are all being answered.

MY INTENTION FOR TODAY IS:

I Intend that the Sweetest Love imaginable, like a torrent of rushing water, washes simultaneously over and through the hearts of every man, woman, and child who walk this Earth. And I Intend, from that moment of Grace forward, that all seven billion of us have a reference point to remind us of how good life can be when we are filled, to the brim, with Love.

A STORY FROM THE PAST

You are the ones to come together and intend a new world.

I remember a time long, long ago; it was mid-evening, the sun already well past the horizon and the full moon had risen over the ridge to the east. We were sitting in a large circle, hundreds of us, spread across a magnificent meadow overlooking the sandy shore fifty feet below. The dolphins played in the reflection of the moonlight as the old woman, her silver hair wafting gently in the warm, tropical trade wind, thanked us for joining her on this historical occasion.

She gestured gracefully with her hands, pointing to each of us in turn, as well as to the moon, the mountaintop, and out toward the vast infinity of ocean in the distance. She gave thanks to everything and everyone for the blessings they were bestowing upon us, and then she quieted for a moment until the wind died down. Now we could hear her words perfectly.

"Today—as you live and breathe here in your beautiful, abundant Lemuria—you enjoy access to riches untold. You experience life at the pinnacle of your culture's evolution, creating at will, masters all of you, living in joy and peace. In recorded history, you can look back for thousands upon thousands of years and you will not find a civilization who has lived, thrived, and reached the levels of individual power and proficiency at manifesting that you have reached. At the same time, your intuitive perceptions have become enhanced to where you now enjoy constant telepathic communication with our fellow travelers who live within the waters. Those of you who are talking regularly with the dolphins, whales, sea turtles, mermen, and mermaids are evolving faster than ever before, as you learn from their teachings about living in alignment with your Highest Good.

"All of these endeavors are to be honored and praised here tonight, for you represent the peak of creative expression that can be achieved by a sentient culture. You have walked upon the waters and flown across the skies. You are the best of your people...and yet, I tell you true, that soon a momentous shift will come upon the land and you will be part of a Great Scattering. Your magical Motherland of Lemuria shall be washed asunder the great waves and her riches tossed in all directions across the ocean floor.

"And you, her once proud and powerful people who were the last to know of a life lived in true peace, will wander from nation to nation, from lifetime to lifetime, through limitation, toil, and suffering unthinkably, looking, searching, and always longing to return and recreate the life you once knew here. And one day, your search shall be rewarded.

"After almost seventy thousand years in your present reckoning of time, a rallying cry will sound. It will come from islands yet to be and resonate deep within you, sparking memories of a time long past; of a time here in this moonlit circle along the shores of Mu, where we made our intentions, agreements, and arrangements to come back together in a place far into the future for the distinct purpose of bringing back the greatness of our beloved Lemuria to the peoples of the Earth.

"The rallying cry that awakens you and sparks you into action is the Highest Good. Those very words—the Highest Good—will find their way across time and space and into your soul, where they will resonate like a song from Heaven. And you will know that that's what you wanted all along— the Highest Good for yourself, for your fellow men and women, and for the world at large. Now, you cannot settle for anything less and you seek out others who are also attracted to the Highest Good. They may call themselves Intenders of the Highest Good, Ascenders of the Highest Good, or perhaps the Unity Highest Good Group. In any case, you will know them and they will know you. You will be lined up together with the Highest Good, and, in time, you will remember the intentions and agreements you made here on this beautiful, tropical night, and you will come back together in the distant future to ring in a new era that will be called the 'Golden Age of God in Manifestation.'"

So, in case you've temporarily forgotten, that is what we came here to do. We came here to be Intenders or Ambassadors of the Highest Good...but we will only be using names like these for a short time. Why? Because we won't need them anymore for we will have turned into Beings of the Highest Good. The Highest Good will have become a way of life again, just like it was back in old Lemuria.

MY INTENTION FOR TODAY IS:

I Intend that I am a Being of the Highest Good.

chapter five

MONEY AND MANIFESTING

OPENING

Each and every person is qualified to have riches.

HERE IS A MESSAGE DIRECTLY FROM TINA AND OUR friend, Lee Ching:

"Each and every person is qualified to have riches. At this time, conscious people, in particular, are opening to their abundance so that the world can be in a better position, and so that the wealth will be shared and there will be much to spare for everyone who needs it. You can do several things to facilitate this process.

First, you will need to open your hearts and your minds to the possibility that you are a divine bringer of money into any situation where it is needed. Be open for magic and miracles and ways of getting money that you never even thought of.

For this to happen, you must begin to look within your own being and search out any blocks to your good. One of these places is in your language. You must be very, very astute with your languaging. You must always speak in a positive manner about money. If you're looking at a rich man and putting him down for his riches, that is a block to your own divine good. Likewise, if you have a block about a given amount—if you are thinking small—then you will be given what you ask for. If you start by asking to expand your ability to receive, to expand your ability to open to larger and larger amounts of money, knowing that you are capable and willing to care and use this money wisely, then you will open to more and more riches being given to you for your work and for your being. It is not only through your work that this money will come, although it is very important to do that which you are here to do. Do what you love and money will come from every direction. Known and unknown sources will open their hands, their minds, and their flow will come to you.

You can also bless the money you already have. To do this you can put a portion of your cash money on a Divine Altar surrounded by Beings that you love and respect. Say to your Divine Beings and to your money, 'I love you. I thank you. I trust you. I enjoy you. And I respect you.' These words go out and focus the energy on your finances. It is that simple. You are blessing your money. You are trusting that you will use it in the right way when you receive it. And, you're respectful of the money and where it is coming from. Divine energy is multiplying your money right now—multiplying it in many ways to give you more and more money to use for the betterment of mankind. Open to this possibility. Open to the generous flow coming to you from places known and unknown. Bless your money and be grateful for what you have. Give thanks for the money that you have, even if it is one dollar. As you are thankful for that one dollar, it will multiply, and zeroes will be added. Many zeroes, and many commas...

Another way to step into your financial abundance is by consciously flowing your money to each other, through the act of tithing, as you have read in the Bible. In this way you flow it to people and places that provide you with your spiritual food. These things are like voting with your money. You are acknowledging your abundance by being open and willing to share your money with those who are giving their gifts to you. Whether it is in the form of work or in the form of spiritual awareness, whatever it might be, as you open to give your money freely, you cause trust to come into your life. When you trust that your money will always be there for you when you need it, then you will be more open and willing to flow your money to others when they are in need, or when they have shared their highest gifts with you.

Remember your gifts. When you give freely of your gifts you will be highly rewarded in every way imaginable. Then all you have to do is ask for what you want. Open for what you deserve. Be a willing and ready receiver for high gifts. Gifts from the Universe. Magical gifts. Miraculous gifts..."

> **MY INTENTION FOR TODAY IS:**
>
> . . . .
>
> *I Intend that I am a Divine Bringer of money into any situation where it is needed.*

ABUNDANCE
. . . .

The source of your supply is so immense.
It's all there just waiting for you to tap into it.

Most people don't realize it, but hoarding always shuts down the flow of our abundance, while giving always comes back to us in great measure. The mechanics of this phenomenon are easily apparent once we get past our old attitudes about "saving for a rainy day." It works like this: when we hoard something, whether it's our money, our time, our resources, or our energy, we're actually doing it because we've pictured ourselves in a situation where we've run out of things. We've envisioned ourselves down and out, perhaps even destitute and depressed. Now, this vision is a thought, and it will work its way into physical manifestation just like any other thought we keep our attention on. In other words, by saving for a rainy day, even though our motivation is to have extra resources for later on, we sabotage our future and create the exact opposite of that which we truly desire for ourselves.

Lee Ching told us one night in our spiritual guidance session that followed our Intenders Circle that it furthers us to bring our limiting thoughts to light so that we can replace them with thoughts that will bring our abundance to us. There's a good example of this, he said, by looking at how the kitchen faucet works. When we open the valve, the water comes in and the water goes out. But when we close off the valve, the water can't come in, so it also cannot flow out. It's the same with our money and our resources; we close off the flow of all good things coming to us by our thoughts of lack and our subsequent acts of hoarding. By the same token, we open the faucet of our abundance and keep it open by spending, not frivolously, but responsibly. When we spend without worrying about it, we send a message to the Universe that we have enough of everything we need, and that we trust that there will always be more when we need it. It's this posture that delivers our abundance to us (if it's for our Highest Good), and provides us with enough to spare and enough to share.

MY INTENTION FOR TODAY IS:

*I Intend that I always have enough
to spare and enough to share.*

THE BIG WAREHOUSE

There is infinite abundance already present.

It serves us immensely to remember that everything comes from the same source. Call it God, the Universe, All That Is, or whatever you like: It is the ultimate Warehouse where everything is stored.

We've been brought up to believe that we need the services of a middleman to deliver our goodies to us. But now, with the advent of the new ways coming to the surface, we are beginning to realize that we can cut out the middlemen and go straight to God with all our requests for the things we desire. From this point on, all we have to do is stay awake and dismiss the limiting thoughts and beliefs that tell us we need someone else other than God. In short, we need to be more confident than ever that the Big Warehouse will ship out whatever we want without the encumbrance of the middlemen who tend to dip their fingers into our pockets along the way.

The middlemen, in their selfishness, have barraged us from the day we were born with all sorts of programming that suggests just how indispensable they are. They erected imaginary barriers between us and the Big Warehouse, and made it sound like the only way we could get the things we wanted was to go through them, the middlemen. At the same time, they also did everything they could to undermine our confidence in the Big Warehouse, even going so far as to make us think that It doesn't exist, or if It does, they are the only ones who have access to It.

They literally planted these limiting, false thoughts in our minds via the media and our classrooms; however, now that many of us are integrating the new ways of thinking into our lives, we are regaining access to the Big Warehouse. After all, who needs a middleman when you can go straight to the source on your own?

You put up a wall between you and your abundance. In this age we are in, there is still a medium of exchange known as money. This will change, but, at this time, you can use it and be open to it and allow it to flow through you. Don't hold onto it or store it up, but be a channel for it to flow into and through you. There is infinite abundance already present. By your thoughts and your words and your deeds, and by your actual stressing and being uptight over it, you are using up the very energy needed for the breakthrough so it can flow to you.

MY INTENTION FOR TODAY IS:

. . . .

I Intend that I am trusting implicitly
that everything I request of God is coming to me
(as long as it serves the Highest Good of myself,
the Universe, and everyone concerned).

EMBRACING UPLIFTMENT

. . . .

We don't have to continue to believe what we were taught
when we were young.

It's all in what we embrace. Those who embrace scarcity shall be subjected to it; those who embrace sickness shall experience its ill effects; those who embrace violence shall perish by it; but those who embrace Love and a caring Spirit shall be embraced by Love in return. What we put out is what we get back. If you find that you've been attracting challenges and discomfort into your life, you can start out by making an intention to be more gentle with yourself from now on.

Whenever you're feeling weak or feeling down, you can draw on the energy and power that comes from the spark that lives deep inside of you, the spark that animates your entire being. Call it up! If you need to sing, sing loudly. If you need to pray, pray loudly. If you need to tone, tone proudly. Do whatever it takes to lift your Spirit so you can look down and see your life, playing itself out. Then you, the person in charge, can watch and decide what is best for you.

Remember that when you lift yourself up, even in the slightest degree, the whole of humanity is lifted up in the same measure. You lift all of humanity up when you reach out for your greatest happiness. Who knows, maybe one day soon you'll cast aside a last lingering belief surrounding your scarcity, sickness, or suffering, and, in that joyous moment of release, it will be just enough for the whole world to breach an ancient barrier and be lifted up to its next level of experience. So be it!

MY INTENTION FOR TODAY IS:

I Intend that I am embracing that which uplifts me and my fellow travelers.

YOUR CALLING

. . . .

Your purpose is to be revealed to you
so that you can spread your wings
and cover this Earth with that which is your creation.

From the time that we were small children, we've been taught to mind our manners and to be like everybody else. We're told that it's respectful of others to practice certain courtesies, and that's fine, as long as we don't become slaves to what other people think or say about us. Taken too far, our conformity keeps us living in a subtle, but very real, state of fear. We become afraid of acting differently than everyone else around us. Even when our hearts tell us to do something one way, our social consciousness screams out to do it another way, lest we draw too much attention to ourselves. And all too often, our fear wins out. To experience our highest calling, we must break the mold. We must do things not as others do, but as our hearts bid us to do.

It helps us to remember that we can have it all. We can have our cake and eat it too. It's entirely possible to combine what is helpful to others with that which is enjoyable to ourselves. The Buddhists call it living our dharma, while in the west we know it best as recognizing and following our calling.

You know when you're following your calling. Everything fits snugly into place. Synchronistic events are everyday fare.

Life gets easy. When you're truly being of service and living your calling, all of the guesswork is removed from your life. You're always in the right place at the right time. You feel different because your body is carrying a higher frequency that attracts others to you. The people you're supposed to be working with always show up, as if by magic. Your whole world becomes a delight to live in because you're committed to doing the work that your soul calls you to do.

It's clear that many of us are realizing that we made an agreement before we came into these bodies, that we would come together at a certain time in order to bring light and love onto this planet and to usher in a golden age. Some have forgotten and some just have a feeling, like an inkling of a long-lost dream, that there really is a reason for us to be here now. In either case, on one level or another, we are all experiencing a movement toward looking at life from the perspective of the soul and the soul group—a perspective of having made agreements and arrangements to come here and meet together with other souls and soul groups and then join together—so that we can assist in raising the vibration of this planet.

This is what is being remembered at this time; and it is this movement that will, in fact, bring the golden age into manifestation.

MY INTENTION FOR TODAY IS:

· ·

*I Intend that I am discovering and doing
what I came here to do.*

SPEAKING IN THE POSITIVE

· ·

*As we replace the negative with the positive,
we see that the results of having made this shift
are filtering down into our daily experiences
where we receive the gifts we truly desire.*

The last word we've eliminated from our vocabulary is *not*.
Our guides told us that our subconscious mind is unable to
recognize the word *not*. Put another way, we were told that
the invisible helpers and angels who work with us to bring our
intentions into manifestation are unable to hear the word *not*
and that things would work out much better for us if we put our
intentions out to the Universe in a positive way. For example,
instead of saying, "I intend that I am not sick anymore," now
we would say, "I intend that I am always in excellent health."
Or, instead of saying, "I intend that I am not afraid anymore,"
we would say, "I intend that I am more courageous."

By saying things in a positive way, our entire lives are becoming more positive. We are subtly empowering ourselves by getting rid of the negatives in our speech.

Integrating positive languaging into your everyday vocabulary may take a little bit of practice. As you become more aware of what you are saying, your old negative habits will tend to surface, and it will be common for you to have to take a few moments to figure out the positive way to say something. This is the same as in your Intenders Circles, where you have often had to help each other find a positive way to phrase an intention. It is good that you have learned to do this because this exercise has served you to become more positive people. You've begun to look upon these instances as opportunities to sharpen your creative abilities. While you've found that it's challenging at times to speak positively, you've also learned that it can be fun as well. That's the spirit with which we in the higher realms recommend you approach positive languaging. Make it fun.

After all, having fun is always a positive thing.

> ## MY INTENTION FOR TODAY IS:
> . . . .
> *I Intend that I am listening closer*
> *to what I am saying,*
> *and that I am eliminating*
> *the negative words from my speech.*

MEDITATION
. . . .

You are your attention.

The greatest battles being fought are not upon the deserts, forests, and fields of Earth but within the human mind. You see, our minds are fair game for anyone who is unscrupulous or unconscious enough to want to take our attention away from us. We are our attention and to the extent that another can get us to put our attention on whatever he or she chooses, we give away a part of ourselves—the most vital part, in fact.

It's interesting that taking someone else's attention away from them has become a widely accepted occurrence in our world today. Most people don't mind at all; they accept that others can interrupt them, regardless of the motivation. Indeed, many people's lives are filled to the brim by constant distraction, and sadly, they never get control over their own attention. That's where meditation comes in. Meditation is the tool we use to regain control over our own mind.

Just before he took his leave, Lee Ching said that a second way to support life is to spend some quiet time alone every day. This idea sounded a little odd to me at first, but the more I thought about it, the more I realized that those who meditate daily are much less likely to become involved in conflicts. Meditators are calmer, less excitable, and more importantly, more apt to see things from a higher perspective. Later on, he told me that this is why those who seek to manipulate us don't want us to meditate because it makes us more difficult to control. Meditators aren't as reliant upon others to tell them what to do because they are cultivating their own inner independence. Compared to most people, they are a lot freer.

> **MY INTENTION FOR TODAY IS:**
>
> *I Intend that I am spending some quiet time by myself every day.*

INVITING

. . . .

Emblazon three little letters
upon your consciousness: A S K.

It is the hallmark of our time that we are all learning to trust at a much deeper level than we have ever had to trust before. And what is it that we're learning to trust in? First, that our thoughts do, indeed, create our world; that what we think about and what we are saying works its way out into our physical environment. Second, that our intentions will, in fact, manifest as we set them. In other words, the laws of manifestation work just fine as long as we apply them and believe in them. And third, a great many of us are learning that there are invisible helpers who will rally to our side if we will but ask.

For, in truth, invisible beings surround us at all times and it is for us to call them forth and ask them to help us with the manifestation of our intentions. Proper directions play a big part in this because there are many invisibles that do not have our highest and best interests at heart and those of us who are working with invisible beings have come to realize that who we call is who will come. In asking or intending that only the Highest Good is served, we close the door on any beings who do not come from a hundred percent pure light.

We highly recommend this short invitation or intention to you for using whenever you're doing anything important and want to make sure that your guidance and helpers stand for the Highest Good.

Feel free to use it as you like. It will make everything simpler for you.

> **MY INTENTION FOR TODAY IS:**
>
> *I Intend that everything needing to be known is known here today; that all of my words are clear, precise, uplifting, helpful, and fun; that each and every one of us here is guided, guarded, and protected throughout this entire experience; and that everything we say and do here today serves the highest and best good of the Universe, ourselves, and everyone everywhere. And so be it and so it is!*

chapter six

LOVE AND GRATITUDE

HIGHER PRIORITIES

Love lets others go first.

THERE IS AN OLD STORY THAT WAS TOLD TO ME by B. J., my first spiritual teacher, which has always inspired me. It has to do with two people, a Master and an Apprentice, who are climbing a ladder together. As they move higher and higher, the Master is leading the way, imparting knowledge and helping the Apprentice overcome obstacles and resistances at almost every rung. Things go on like this for quite awhile until they finally reach the top rung of the ladder. At this point, the Master stops, leans aside to make room for the Apprentice to pass, and says, "Here, my friend, you go first."

In today's fast-paced, workaday world, many of us have a tendency to charge ahead, not always thinking about how we affect our fellow travelers. Our economic and social systems aren't currently geared for helpfulness to blossom. Whether we scramble blindly to make our monthly obligations, or simply cut another off in traffic in a rush to get to our next place quicker, we lose a special opportunity to have a positive effect on those around us and on ourselves. Just think for a moment how you reacted the last time someone else slowed at an intersection and waved for you to go ahead of them. It felt good, didn't it? You wanted to return the favor, didn't you?

That's the way we'll all feel once we glean the wisdom in allowing others to go first.

MY INTENTION FOR TODAY IS:

I Intend that I am more willing to consider the needs of those around me.

LEARNING TO LOVE BETTER

. . . .

*All things are moving toward that which
you are moving toward.*

Whenever the hustle and bustle of life starts to weigh heavily upon you, and your mind seems to run around in never-ending circles, one of the quickest ways to rebalance yourself is to make a connection with the Earth. Go out and get your bare feet on the lawn or in the sand at the beach. Just as your TV reception will clear up when you run a wire from the antenna to the ground, so shall your thoughts and feelings smooth out when you connect with Mother Earth. It's one of the easiest ways for you to love yourself.

In fact, there are many ways of learning to love, not only yourself, but those around you, as well. Another is to plant and grow some food of your own. Most people don't realize it, but something very special happens when we nurture and consume food that we have grown for ourselves. Not only does the life force in it transfer to us when we eat it, the love that we put into caring for it has a magical way of returning to us from Mother Earth herself. Indeed, she befriends all those who care for the least of her creatures.

And it doesn't matter whether it's an acre of organic gardens you're growing or a single kumquat tree or tomato plant you keep on the patio. It can even be a batch of sprouts (for those who want the quickest results) that live on your kitchen windowsill. Regardless of what you plant, you will have shortened the gap between you and your food supply by being just that much less reliant on someone else to provide you with your food. It is a subtle shift, but one that raises your Spirit the minute you cover the little seeds over with soil and water them.

Back on the farm, B. J. used to say that if we wanted to learn to love better, it would be a good idea for us to start out with plants. Plants are the easiest, he said, because they stay in one place and hold still when we're working with them. They also have a way of reflecting the love we give them back at us right away by perking up when we water them, and greening up quickly when we fertilize. And, they won't hurt us if we accidentally harm them (unless, of course, we get too close to the ones with thorns!).

After we get the hang of taking care of plants, and they are thriving happily under our supervision, we can go on to animals. Animals, he said, are a little trickier to love because they move around. Unlike plants, it's more difficult to get them to do things they don't want to do. Oh yeah, and they also make their share of noises and messes that will sometimes surprise us.

Then, after we get pretty good at taking care of plants and

animals, we can move on to learning how to love people better. According to B. J., people are much harder to love because not only do they move around and make messes, but they'll talk back, change their minds, be unloving in return, and do all sorts of things that will challenge our patience. They'll even bring out the worst in us (often by unknowingly providing the adversity we need the most), and sometimes, he said, it can take years before we see the results of our love.

Conversely, he also stated that they can bring out the best in us. This usually happens when we've matured enough ourselves to the point where we are able to set aside all of our personal reactions to their adversities, noises, messes, and so forth, and see into the core of who they really are. That's when we really learn to love. And ironically, that's also when our love comes back to us.

MY INTENTION FOR TODAY IS:
. . . .

I Intend that I am deliberately learning to love,
that life is my teacher, and my everyday
experiences are the perfect lessons
I need to move forward.

GETTING HOME

. . . .

See the essence of divinity in every person.

We get asked a lot about the First Intent of The Code where it says to refrain from opposing anyone. People seem to have a hard time wrapping their minds around the idea that it's possible to go through our days without opposing others. They say they can't imagine living without opposition, but we say that the human being is an inherently warm, trusting, affectionate type who has become colder due to the influence of outside forces. We are not naturally predisposed to be violent; it is something we were taught to do, and now we have to unlearn our violent ways by looking deeper into how they are really affecting us.

Every judgment we make works against us. Every opposition we create boomerangs back to blindside us eventually, often in ways we least expect. Throughout these reminders we have repeatedly talked about the idea that when we oppose someone we are becoming just like them. Perhaps we neglected, however, to also point out the complete and utter futility of our opposition.

Opposition always leaves us empty; it always leaves a mess behind for us to clean up. People suffer and die in its wake, never to fulfill the calling they set for themselves in this life. In truth, opposition never achieves its "suggested" result of making peace or providing the way for a better life for everyone. Quite the contrary, it only fans the flames of the other person's hatred and makes them want to retaliate. Said another way, opposing, in every instance, brings the exact opposite result from that which we truly desire. It's like deciding we're going to drive to the store in town, but turning the wrong way out of the driveway, and then wondering why we aren't getting where we want to go. It's a self-perpetuating dead-end cycle, an exercise in futility. Opposition creates more opposition. It's a Universal Law.

So how do we stop the hatred and the war? There is only one way. Love. We can learn to love our enemies, and to give them the respect they deserve as fellow travelers who seek, just as we seek, to have a better life and to enjoy all the abundance that the Earth sets before us. We can ask them how we can help them instead of looking for ways to harm them. We can set a good example by withdrawing our swords immediately, whether they are the swords of war, or the swords of daily judgment toward our neighbors and coworkers. Then, and only then, will we feel what it's like to be at home on Planet Earth. Then, and only then, can we begin to get reacquainted with the rest of our Earthly family, the other eight billion souls who want only for the same comforts we do. Love is the only stance that will bring us home.

MY INTENTION FOR TODAY IS:

. . . .

*I Intend that I am doing whatever
I have to do to love my enemies.*

FINDING YOUR HEART

. . . .

*It is good to explore that which is coming
to you from within.*

It always seems strange to me to go to a sporting event in a large stadium or auditorium and when they play the National Anthem almost everyone in the crowd stands up and holds their hands over their hearts, on the left side of their chests. The same thing happens when you go into a classroom today and see the children saying the Pledge of Allegiance to the flag while holding their hands over a spot on the left side of their chests, thinking that that is where their hearts are.

But wait a minute! That's not where our heart is at all. Our heart is in the exact center of our chest. No matter what the doctors, teachers, sports enthusiasts, or the children tell you, your heart is in the middle, just as if your body is aligned on a cross. The exact center point where the horizontal and vertical points meet is where the heart of your heart sits.

I've even spoken with young children about this and they will swear that their heart is on the left side, and when I asked them how they knew that to be true, they said that their teacher told them so.

So what is the purpose in deceiving so many people from a very young age about the correct placement of their heart? It is because our heart is a very special focal point. It is where we connect to all the Love in the Universe. However, if we can't find it, or think it is somewhere where it isn't, then it becomes harder for us to come into contact with the true Love of God. And it is much easier for us to be controlled.

It sounds crazy, but, on a very subtle level, when we lose track of the location of our heart, it becomes more difficult for us to send and receive Love. For thousands of years the powers that be have conspired to keep our hearts hidden from us so they could keep us anchored to the Earth where it is easier to manipulate us. But now we are beginning to see through all of the deceptions that are constantly being perpetrated upon humanity, and we are finding our hearts and all the Love that resides there. For it is in the center of our heart where all of the things we search for, where all of the treasures we travel far and wide to find, where all of the successes we toil for lifetimes to achieve, where the most sacred sites and the sweetest feelings available to us can be found. For those who are still skeptical, I suggest that you hold your undivided attention on the center of your chest for a while and see what happens.

> ## MY INTENTION FOR TODAY IS:
> . . . .
> *I Intend that I am remembering to place my attention in the center of my heart every day.*

GRATITUDE
. . . .

Go forth with Gratitude and all is added unto you.

Gratitude is what makes the Intention Process work. It's the acknowledgment that the intentions we've made in the past have come true. When we express our gratitude, we're saying thank you to the Universe for bringing us the things that we've asked for. We're saying that we recognize that a connection exists between ourselves and the Universe, we appreciate this connection, and know that we can call on it at any time.

There is always a lot of gratitude expressed in our Intenders Circles. In fact, that's what our Intenders Circles are for: to make our intentions and to express our gratitude for their manifestation. When an Intender speaks of gratitude, it shows everyone in the circle that the laws of manifestation work. It gives those who still carry doubts and skepticism a newfound confidence and heightens their level of trust when they see their fellow Intenders "winning."

And that's how it all starts. We make an intention, and soon, when it has manifested, we feel like we've gotten a win and we say so by stating our gratitude. The Intention Process has come full circle. It started out with an intention and it ended with a statement of gratitude.

Once we've seen ourselves and our friends get a win or two, it gets much easier for all of us. We put even more trust in the Intention Process and then we get more and more wins. Pretty soon, we're winning all of the time! Eventually, we'll look around us and see that the world we're living in is the one we've intended for ourselves. We will have created everything in our world consciously. When enough of us have done this, others will learn from our example, and we will all begin to walk this Earth free and full of gratitude.

"Last spring, during the potluck at an Intenders meeting, a very successful woman was telling us about how she manifests things. She was using money as an example. She said that she was grateful for it, both before and after it arrives. That got me started thinking. Up until then, money was always a challenge for me. Every time a bill would come in the mail, I would get upset. Right away, I would start to complain and I'd walk around muttering and wondering how I was ever going to pay it. But since that meeting, I've started doing something different. Now, I thank the Universe when I get a bill in the mail. I think of all the wonderful things that the bills are providing for me and I'm really grateful for them.

Needless to say, everything is much better financially for me now. Since I've started being grateful, I've received more money than I ever had before. It just keeps flowing in, like water from the kitchen faucet. Sometimes I'm even pleasantly surprised by where it comes from!"

—RON MERRIWEATHER

MY INTENTION FOR TODAY IS:

I Intend that I am living in grace and gratitude.

THE BIGGER PICTURE

Truly, life is immortal. There is no beginning and no end.

Every now and then, when I feel myself starting to get a little restless, I ponder the bigger picture for a while. The first thought that usually comes to mind is that this Earthly existence is but one reality out of an infinite number of realities I could have chosen to take part in. Then I think that out of all the possible scenarios available to me, this one is just about as interesting and exciting as it gets.

What other place could I have entered as innocent and helpless as this one? Where else could I find the beauty and diversity of Beings as are here on the Earth? And where else offers the challenges which, according to the Mayan calendar, include not only a total shift in this lifetime in the way humanity thinks and acts, but also a much larger shift in the whole cosmos that is almost unimaginable in its breadth and scope? Truly, we sit on the cusp of an age where anything can happen!

I don't know about you, but I feel very grateful to be here. Even when things aren't going my way, I look around and can't help but think what a beautiful place this is and how amazing it is that I get to be here at this time to unravel the wondrous mysteries of life.

Once we've taken heart and learned to trust in our power, the next step is to stretch our imagination and know that we can create anything that we can think of. When we go beyond the bounds of our old, consensus reality, whole new realms open up before us. We can have leaders who are kind and beneficent; we can clean our air and water in a matter of days; we can enjoy free energy, free food, free shelter, free everything! A life of total comfort is available to anyone who is willing to shed their old thinking processes.

MY INTENTION FOR TODAY IS:

I Intend that I feel blessed to be here.

chapter seven

RELATIONSHIPS

THE HIGHEST GOOD AGAIN

What we ask for is what we get.

EARLIER, WE SAID THAT THERE WERE THREE things that kept our intentions from manifesting: our doubts, the timing (yet) factor, and the Highest Good. When we were first starting the Intenders back on the Big Island of Hawaii, Mark Dziatko (he's the handsome one in the Intenders video) and I used to talk a lot about the Highest Good. One day while we were putting a roof on his house in Waa Waa subdivision, Mark was telling me why some of the things I'd manifested recently didn't seem to be working out so well. He said I hadn't incorporated the Highest Good into my intentions. Mark said that this was a common oversight, and he pointed out that there are all sorts of things we think we want, but that sometimes it's difficult for us to tell in advance which ones are good for us and which ones aren't. He said that we can avoid getting ourselves involved in uncomfortable situations by including the Highest Good clause at the end of our intentions.

He further explained that by saying "in order for my intentions to manifest, they must serve the Highest Good of the Universe, myself, and everyone everywhere," (and knowing that what I say is what I'll get), I can be assured that only the intentions which are aligned with my Highest Good will come into manifestation. Any which are born out of shadowy, selfish, or unserving motives will remain unmanifested.

We had an example of this in our Intenders Circle with a lady named Genie who kept making the same intention week after week. She intended that she is in a relationship with the man of her dreams, and, week after week, we expected her to arrive at the circle with her new boyfriend on her arm. But, after several months, it still hadn't happened.

So, one evening after we'd finished our intentions and gratitudes, Mark asked Lee Ching why Genie's intention hadn't manifested yet. The answer he received was quite profound. He was told that it simply wasn't in Genie's (or her future boyfriend's) highest and best interests to have a man come into her life at this time; that she didn't really have the handle on her negativity yet; and that if he was to show up in her life, she wouldn't be able, at her present level of emotional maturity, to keep him around. It was suggested that she do some more work on herself to keep calmer and more centered in the midst of life's little storms, and, in this way, when the man of her dreams did come along, she'd be better prepared to make the most of the relationship.

> **MY INTENTION FOR TODAY IS:**
> ....
> *I Intend that all of my intentions serve the Highest Good of the Universe, myself, and everyone everywhere.*

NEGATIVE EMOTIONS
. . . .

Nothing good can ever come from a negative emotion.

Most people are unaware of the effects of their negative emotions. Not only do these emotions—anger, hatred, sorrow, self-pity, greed, worry, grief, and so forth—do us no good whatsoever in our lives, when expressed, they always make matters worse. Indeed, they are the chief contributors to the aging process, and if we would refrain, for a time, from indulging in them, our youth would begin to return and we would rejuvenate.

But these things are not taught in school. Instead, we've been taught to guard and protect our right to feel sorrowful, for instance. We feel grief over the parting or loss of a loved one, never realizing that nothing positive can ever come from our grief, that feeling bad is a lower manifestation that opens us up to all sorts of unwanted repercussions. We simply do not realize that grief, worry, sorrow, self-pity, and so on have the effect of weakening our body's immune system and aging us prematurely. If we truly knew how much we harm ourselves, not to mention others, when we act out our negative emotions, we would reevaluate our behavior immediately.

Our negative reactions have never had one positive effect on anyone, ever! Unfortunately, most people think, for example, that it's fine and dandy to hate others, and that if someone else does something hateful to us we are perfectly justified, even obligated, to hate or harm them back. The simple truth, however, is that not only do our negative emotions harm us personally, they actually make every situation worse because they feed the flames of our enemy's anger and make them want to retaliate all the more. Our negativity catches us in a vicious cycle from which there is only one way out.

The only way to defuse our arguments, hatreds, and wars is to love our opponents. Love removes the negative charge from our conflicts, leaving them to disappear and disintegrate due to lack of sustenance. The fires of hatred and war automatically die out when we stop feeding them.

B. J. used to liken our negative emotional reactions to the way Velcro works. He said that when you look real close, Velcro has a whole bunch of tiny hooks that catch and hold fast to thousands of little eyes. He explained further that when someone else is angry and yelling at us, if we react it is because they hooked into our own fear and anger. But, if we are committed to loving them, it's like we've sanded or smoothed off all of the little eyes so there isn't any way for them to get their hooks in us. Our arguments would fade away because there is no negative reaction for someone else to grab onto. There is only love.

MY INTENTION FOR TODAY IS:

*I Intend that I am catching myself
before expressing my next negative emotion
and that I am acting out of love instead.*

BACKBITING

. . . .

Pretend you're above it,
looking down from a mountaintop.

It's real easy nowadays to find yourself in conversations where people are talking about other people, saying things they probably wouldn't say if the other person was there. What most people don't understand is that gossiping has the same effect on those we talk about that sickness does. It works against them. Just as when we talk about Aunt Flora's bad knees and, in doing so, we make her knees worse, so do we make things worse for people we backbite. But with backbiting, there is an added detriment: we make things worse for ourselves, as well.

It works like this: If we are talking about a neighbor, for instance, it is because we've first been entertaining thoughts about that person. As you're learning, thoughts are invisible but very potent, nonetheless. And they are received—always— by whomever we're thinking about. So, if we're thinking about being wronged by our neighbor, we are actually reinforcing our neighbor's "wrongful" behavior. We're adding to it, and here's the kicker: If, when we are backbiting or gossiping about the neighbor, or we are standing in opposition to them in any way, we are also becoming just like them.

You've seen this often. When someone is complaining about another person you know, if you look closely, you can see them beginning to act just like the person they're complaining about.

The best thing to remember in these situations is that we become like whomever (or whatever) we place our attention upon. It's the Law, whether we are aware of it or not. Once we truly understand that we're becoming like the person we're backbiting—and that we are also reinforcing their discordant behavior—shouldn't that give us pause to reconsider our own actions?

The deepest desire of every one of us is to know that we are loved, to know that our world will feed us and give us all that we need just as it freely surrounds us with the air we breathe, the water we drink, the land we walk upon. Constantly giving to us like a parent to a child.

We harm ourselves and others in ways we don't realize when we backbite or gossip. Wouldn't it be better if we were to use our precious time and energy on a creative endeavor that fulfills us and makes us happier? And what would happen if, instead of giving in to our fears of lack and losing (which is why we gossip in the first place), we were to think kindly thoughts of our neighbors? That's what will give us the results we truly desire for ourselves.

MY INTENTION FOR TODAY IS:

. . . .

I Intend that I am rising above any behavior
that isn't serving me and my fellow travelers.

RENEWING

. . . .

To renew yourself,
you need to take a break every so often.

Anything we do repetitively for too long a time causes us to
grow stale. It doesn't matter whether it's at our job, eating
the same food, driving the same car, or in our relationships,
if we stay at it without taking an occasional break, we are
confronted by the Law of Diminishing Returns. Simply put,
the Law of Diminishing Returns says that you can eat one ice
cream cone and it's good; you can eat two ice cream cones
and they're still good; but if you go on to eat seven or eight ice
cream cones, you'll start to get pretty uncomfortable. You'll
need to take a break from ice cream for a while and renew
yourself so that you can come back and eat ice cream cones
again in the near future.

This little analogy not only works for ice cream cones, but

for everything we do. We become inefficient and dull if we do not work with this law consciously.

I had a very good friend in Kona who worked side by side throughout the week with his wife, and he always made a deliberate point to get away every second or third weekend to watch sports on TV with his buddies. Needless to say, his wife was not always happy about this, especially because he would just up and go whenever he felt that their relationship was becoming strained by their being so close together all the time. But, in the long run, their relationship flourished year in and year out because he had the wisdom to work in harmony with the Law of Diminishing Returns and get away so that they would both have the time to recharge and come back together, renewed.

MY INTENTION FOR TODAY IS:

I Intend that I am working consciously with the Law of Diminishing Returns and that I am taking a break when I need it.

THE CHILDREN

Our children are the seeds of love returning.

Take good care of your children. Many of the children being born at this time carry gifts that will change the way all future generations experience their lives. They bring an expansion of awareness with them. It is time for certain energies to be grounded, so to speak, and the children who are here and also those who are coming into their bodies now will remove limitations from your lives. They are the children of the stars who will act as catalysts for the ushering in of a new world. They are the seeds of love returning.

We have great need of their gifts, for as more and more people begin to love, instead of fearing and hating each other, we reach ever closer toward achieving a freedom and fulfillment in our lives that knows no bounds. One moment, domination and exploitation are the order of the day, and, in the very next moment, the loving words of a child, a child such as the one you see around you every day, may be whispered, and a healing transformation will happen to the last person in a long chain. This person, in finding their love, will be instrumental in birthing the critical mass that your Spirit has longed for.

Indeed, when enough people have returned to love, a long-awaited shift will occur that causes the old ways that have ruled the people on the surface of this Earth for ages upon ages to vanish in the blink of an eye and be replaced by a peace and a grace that will last throughout all of eternity.

And it can all start with a child.

MY INTENTION FOR TODAY IS:

*I Intend that I am treating the children
I meet as if they are the most beautiful gifts
I could ever receive.*

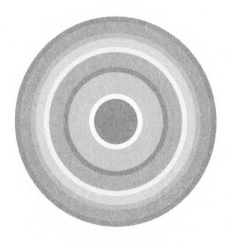

chapter eight

NATURE

OUR MOTHER EARTH

*The Earth is a live entity and she responds
to you as you respond to her.*

I LOVE MOTHER EARTH. I CAN'T TELL YOU WHY, I
just do. She's part of my calling, my purpose for being here,
and somewhere along the line I realized that I'm supposed to
leave her in better shape than I found her.

That's what the Native Americans of old did. When they
left a place where they had been living, regardless of whether
it was overnight or over the season, you couldn't even tell they
had been there. In other words, they cleaned up behind themselves. Wouldn't it be great if we all learned to clean up behind
ourselves? Wouldn't it be great if we began to notice how nice
it is when we come into an area and it's pristine, beautiful,
and inviting because the previous inhabitants took the time to

clean it up? When you've moved into a new home where the previous owner took really good care of it and cleaned it thoroughly for you, weren't you appreciative? Didn't you respect them for considering you, the next people to live there?

Leaving our environment as clean as we found it is a trait that's largely been forgotten in our world today. This pertains not only to our homes and campsites, but to our entire Earth as well. We're leaving it to our children. Wouldn't it be nice if we left them a place that is better than we found it? Wouldn't they be more apt to look back upon us with respect and gratitude for the good works we had done?

But, of course, that is generally not what is happening in today's world. We are busy making messes—environmental, nuclear, economic, political, poverty-ridden, battle-strewn messes—as fast as we can. Clearly, when we wake up and truly care again for our Earth and all her inhabitants, one of the very first things we will do is clean up our messes, beginning with our own backyards and moving outward from there. It will be a glorious day when we see people coming out of their homes and gathering together to clean up the streets and grounds in their own neighborhoods, picking up the scraps of paper and cans and plastic that we take for granted today. To me, some of the greatest heroes of our time are the ones you see with black plastic bags slung over their shoulders, walking along the streets, roads, beaches, and byways bending over and picking up the trash. There is a man who walks Torrey Pines Beach in San Diego every day doing just that. He is as tan, healthy, and vital as it gets, and I am sure that nobody pays him to do it. Because of him, the beach is one of the prettiest in the world and people flock to it to experience the feeling of natural beauty that is there. He is my hero.

I think the main cause for our mess-making mentality is that we've forgotten that Mother Earth is alive. We tend to get so caught up in our work and in our own minds that we neglect to look around and see that, like us, she is a living, breathing creature who wants only for the well-being of herself and her children. And, like us, she feels and responds to her immediate environment based on her ideals. She wants to grow and glow and thrive and evolve to her highest potential, no different than we do. It is a great truth that when we begin to help her in earnest—even if it's to bend over and pick up a piece of paper from the side of the road—she will see to it that our lives are made all the better because of what we have done on her behalf. She will help us as we help her.

Look at nature. Nature is filled with wheat fields. Nature is filled with fruit trees. Nature is filled with all its gifts. It is abundant in every way. You are a willing receiver of these fruits, of these gifts. In return, is it too much to ask for you to give your blessings to the Earth Mother? She needs them.

She needs them right now. Dance on her. Drum on her. Love on her. She needs you. She needs your love, your respect, your trust. She needs you to enjoy her. Give her lots of love, for she has been ignored to the nth degree. Your buildings—not one of them is as beautiful as one of her mountains. See with your eyes the beauty she has given to you; that she gives you every single day. Give her love and attention and she will give it back to you in countless ways, in ways that you can barely imagine...

MY INTENTION FOR TODAY IS:

. . . .

I Intend that I am creating a world
that is always in support of me.

NATURE

. . . .

Feel freer to go into nature when you need to.

Remember back when you used to go camping? It was great fun. You packed up the car with all the goodies and headed for the hills. You slept in tents and took walks among the trees and went swimming in the lakes and streams. Remember how good the food tasted, even when it was slightly charred. After dinner, you'd throw on a couple more logs and sit around the campfire under the stars and tell stories you wouldn't tell if you were back home.

Some folks could camp with a bag of trail mix granola, a sleeping bag, and a few lightweight miscellaneous items. And some folks would load the station wagon to the gills with everything but the washer and dryer. Both systems work fine. Either method can adapt itself to becoming a pleasant lifestyle.

Remember, camping is one of the most fun things we do. It is a leisure-time activity. In fact, given the choice, some of us might approach camping as if we were going on a spree. Our own personal Camporama Jamboree. Load up the coolers with all the food we've got. Bring the tents and tarps and plenty of ropes and wood-cutting tools. And don't forget the camp stove, so we don't have to build a wood fire before having our morning coffee. Throw all the blankets and clothing in doubled trash bags and after that, bring on the toys, books, stereos, solar TV, games, musical instruments, you name it. We've been known to take an extra tent just for all the goodies.

Most campsites tend to sprawl out after awhile. We usually start with a small nucleus of a couple of tents and a picnic table and grow outward from there. Every time we go anywhere, we keep our eye out for practical materials. You'd be surprised how wonderfully useful some old item you found along the roadside becomes when you take it back to camp. Things you need, but never thought you'd find, suddenly pop up and ask you to carry them home. Sometimes a simple stick or a tree limb will be just the ticket. And finding it can give you the same satisfaction you used to get from buying several bags of stuff from the hardware store.

We adapt. We find joy in the little things. We make use of everything. We relax and return to life out-of-doors, camping. And once we get food, water, warm, and dry taken care of, let the spree begin. Put up the banner. Pop a cold drink. Break out the marshmallows. Light the campfire and listen to it crackle. Smell the soup as it bubbles in the iron kettle. Stir your senses alive in the crisp night air. Don't hold back now. Go for it! It's time for the Jamboree!

MY INTENTION FOR TODAY IS:

I Intend that I am getting outdoors more often.

BEAUTY

· · · · · · · · · · ·

*If you're driving down the road and you see
only beautiful flowers, and your neighbor is driving
down the same road and sees only weeds,
who is right? What you are tuned into,
that's what you create for yourself.*

It's interesting how some of us are so readily inclined to see the dark side of things, even when we are surrounded by extraordinary beauty. We complain out of habit, thinking, often unconsciously, that we'll receive some nice reward for all our grumbling. Unfortunately, we may get our treat, but we will also have to live out the results of our complaining, and thus miss out on some of the greatest gifts Mother Earth has to offer. For it's when we hold our attention on her beauty, that something special is called up within us; something that instinctively makes us want to take good care of the Earth. From that point on, we clearly see where our greatest rewards are coming from. They come from taking care of that which is taking care of us.

We go camping a lot and have since we were little children. Our parents used to pack up the station wagon on Friday evenings and drive my brothers and sisters and me out to the woods. Our favorite place was about twenty miles from town in a grove of trees that bordered a beautiful oblong lake. There weren't many people camping around us back then, but now, since it is so lovely, it's packed all weekend long. In the old days, we used to hunt in the nearby woods. We didn't see how special it was, so we'd kill all kinds of animals, chop the trees and bushes indiscriminately, dump stuff in the water, and leave a big mess behind when we went home. It didn't matter to us back then.

Somewhere along the line, though, we made a conscious intention to remember just how sacred it was to be out in nature. I don't remember exactly how it came about, but, over time, we gained an appreciation for the lake and the forest that we didn't have before. We slowed our pace down and began to approach our time in nature more lightly, more gently. We started cleaning up after ourselves so you couldn't tell we'd been there. And we stopped killing the animals, and if, by accident, we harmed an animal or a plant, we did like the Native Americans, and we thanked it for its gift to us.

That's when we noticed the change. It started to feel better out by the lake. Animals who used to run and hide when we were around began coming right up to us. Any firewood that we needed was always nearby. And, beyond all of that, a feeling of peace is there now that wasn't there before. Even though we have a lot more activity around us, our little campsite is so peaceful that other campers always stop by and remark about it.

All said and done, we have a much better time out by the

lake now that we take care of it, instead of harming it. And sometimes late at night, when I lay in my sleeping bag and look up at the stars, I feel so good I never want to leave.

MY INTENTION FOR TODAY IS:

. . . .

I Intend that I am taking good care
of Mother Earth.

DRAMAS

. . . .

That which is meant to be yours will come to you.

So many people's lives today are filled with dramas and unresolved situations that we would like to show you two ways we have found to lessen their effects upon you and your friends. In the early days of the Intenders, we used to say that we share our dreams instead of our dramas. However, it isn't always the way we do things nowadays. On evenings when our Intenders Circle is smaller and we have more time to state our gratitudes and intentions, we will encourage those who are experiencing a sticky situation or drama to talk about it for a short time.

We've found that when we do this for a minute or two

the Intender will open up and get clearer about what's bothering them. Then we'll ask them to state an intention around the drama and do you know what happens? Almost without exception, they'll come back to the Circle a couple of weeks later and the drama is gone. The intention they made manifested, and the drama went away.

In order for you to see things from a higher ground, you must learn to detach from suffering and drama. The faster you can learn to do whatever it takes to lift yourself up and out of dramatic situations, the better it will be for you and for all those around you. If you need to go out the door and shut it behind you and say, "I'm not going back there for a day or two," then do that. If you're in a situation at work where you're feeling really drained and you need to regenerate, go out into nature. Nature is there for you. It is filled with vital life and energy. Avail yourself of it. It is your birthright, as a human being, to be with the trees, the wind, the sun, and the rain. These things add unto you. They regenerate you. They recreate you.

MY INTENTION FOR TODAY IS:
. . . .
I Intend that I am at peace within myself.

CEREMONY
. . . .

Ceremony ignites the spark of enthusiasm. It ignites
the light of willpower. It gives man the strength
to carry on, to move forward,
to have motivation.

When you get into one of those moods where you feel like you
can't make a difference or like your life is out of control, you
can always turn to ceremony to give you a boost. Indeed, that's
one of the great things about ceremony: it catapults you up and
out of your apathy. It ignites the spark of willpower within
you. Ceremony is like medicine for the lost soul.

Of course, an Intenders Circle is an easy, empowering ceremony that is guaranteed to bring you out of your doldrums.
What could be simpler than getting a few of your friends
together, sitting in a circle, saying what you're grateful for, and
what you intend out loud into the circle, dedicating it all to
the Highest Good, and doing a Oneness exercise when you're

done? Your apathy doesn't stand a chance, especially once your intentions have begun to manifest for you.

Many cultures have wonderful ceremonial traditions, not the least of which are the Native American tribes. They offer so many sacred ceremonies, in fact, that you can choose among many of them.

Just before Mark, Tina, Betsy, and I started the Intenders, I had been living in Hawaiian Acres, putting together a piece of property and making it my home. I was living alone and life had gotten into a routine that was dictated by the rains that came down the mountain every afternoon, leaving me to hang out in my little coffee shack reading or just thinking most of the time.

Almost on a whim, I decided to take a few of the large rocks that were left over from a retaining wall I'd just finished building and make a Medicine Wheel in my backyard. I placed them in a perfect circle, just like the Native Americans, and began to walk around the wheel every day. I asked, while I walked, for an acceleration of my spiritual evolution (and, as I said, right after that the Intenders were born).

I tested several different ceremonies to see which ones I liked the best, and eventually settled on the one I still use today, which was taught to me by a Kahuna from South Point, who used it to purify the people who came to him for healing.

Since it's had such a beneficial effect on me, I'll share it with you now.

I enter the Medicine Wheel from the East, giving thanks, calling forth the Highest Good, and asking permission to walk. If it doesn't feel right I don't walk that day, but that is very rare. Then I walk around the inside perimeter of the stones clockwise five times: the first time (as I walk), thanking and blessing the Holy Father; the second time, thanking and blessing the Divine Mother; the third time, thanking and blessing all of God's Holy Angels; the fourth time, thanking and blessings all Beings everywhere; and the fifth time, thanking and blessing myself.

When I've finished my fifth walk around the wheel, I end up in the exact center, facing East, and I say my Intentions. Sometimes I envision a pillar of light going up from the Medicine Wheel and that my Intentions are broadcast out from it to the Universe. I always give thanks to Great Spirit/God/The Highest Good (your choice) again before I exit the wheel at the same place I came in from.

Another variation of this, if you don't have enough space for building a Medicine Wheel in your yard, is to become your own priest or priestess. Start out by getting some real salt, not the standard table salt, but some Himalayan or Celtic or Red Hawaiian Ala'e salt. Now draw yourself a nice warm bath. Before you get in, however, kneel down beside the tub and swirl the water clockwise five times with your hand, each time blessing it in the name of 1) the Holy Father, 2) the Divine Mother, 3) All God's Holy Angels, 4) All Beings everywhere, and 5) Yourself. Then, add five pinches of salt to the bath-water, each time blessing and making your dedications like you did when you swirled the water. Now, get into the bath and soak as long as you like.

Before you get out, give thanks again and say, "I ask that anything unlike Love, anything unlike God, leaves my body now and goes into this water, and (as you get up and pull the stopper from the tub) that it goes down the drain and into the Earth to be purified and transmuted into its highest and best use."

Now...you've just become a priest or priestess. You've made a tubful of Holy Water and soaked in it to your heart's delight. One thing is certain. After you get out of a tub like this, you'll feel better than you've felt in a long time.

MY INTENTION FOR TODAY IS:

I Intend that whenever I feel encumbered or apathetic I am using ceremony to purify myself.

COMMON SENSE REVISITED

. . . .

It is not wise to destroy that which takes care of you.

As we apply the Ninth Intent of The Code by envisioning, and thus beginning to create our ideal world, one of the first things that will go by the wayside is the use of nuclear energy. We simply won't be needing nuclear energy in the golden age we are stepping into, and so we might as well begin by getting rid of all nuclear devices right now.

That even includes the use of X-rays. Some people say, "Well, it's okay for us to use radiation for X-rays, but we don't want it for larger purposes," but they're missing the point. Radiation in any form is debilitating on the human body. It harms more than it helps. We've been conditioned to believe that X-rays allow us the only view into the physical body, however this is not true. There are many who are psychic now who can use their talents to look inside the body to help their fellow man. And there are many more who are on the verge of realizing their psychic skills if they would but develop their abilities.

So, let's be even clearer. We don't need nuclear energy for anything, and we never did. The use of nuclear energy is a lot more serious than we have been led to believe. We've been told that bringing it into an area will bolster a sagging economy, or provide more jobs, or spread around a few more million dollars, but at what cost? Is it really worth it?

Our saving grace lies in our intuition. We have to learn to trust our inner feelings about things like this. We know, for example, that nuclear energy is dangerous, and yet we continue to take it so lightly, like it is nothing to bring some Cobalt-60 into a neighborhood to irradiate our food. Or, it is nothing to build a nuclear power plant right next to a populated beach. Something just doesn't feel right about that.

Please understand that it is not my purpose to talk about gloom and doom here. I'm simply saying that our priorities are way out of whack. We don't need nuclear energy, and it's time to do something about it. Along with practicing the Ninth Intent of The Code we can demand of our leaders that all the research on free energy that's been hidden for decades be made public and implemented as soon as possible; we can begin to replace all nuclear power plants with hydroelectric and any of the many other alternatives available to us; and we can begin dismantling every nuclear weapon on this Earth immediately, and not stop until all of them are gone forever.

That is my firm intention. In fact, let's take it a step further. My inner guidance assures me that when I am in need of turning any doubts, negative thoughts, and/or dark energies around, the most proficient way of doing so is to call in help from the higher realms and command these dark things away with all the inner strength I can muster. So I'm going to do that now:

I Intend, in the name of all God's Holiest Angels and

the Highest Good, that all nuclear energies depart from this planet now and that all nuclear weaponry is dismantled and ceases to exist upon this Earth as of this moment. Be Gone Now! Do you align with me?

So be it and so it is.

MY INTENTION FOR TODAY IS:

I Intend that I am living in a perfectly pristine, healthy, and safe environment.

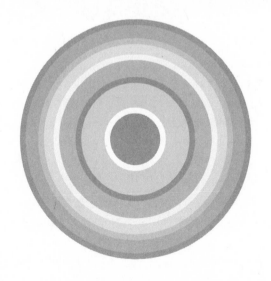

chapter nine

ADVERSITY

STAYING UPLIFTED

*Oftentimes things may be happening all around you
that seem to be discordant, and you cannot imagine
what is going on. But you must remain
focused and steadfast and be able to see through
and not get caught up in the mundane dramas
that are constantly being perpetuated on this planet.*

I HAVE GOOD FRIENDS WHO LIVE WAY OUT IN
the desert in order to get away from everything. Like a lot
of people nowadays, the husband is obsessed with disasters
and potential catastrophes. In fact, he even has a cave on his
land stocked with enough survival goodies to feed and water a
small town. I lived with my friends for a few months the winter
before last, and every day, as we worked together, the husband
would talk about last night's Art Bell radio show, and he even
taped the most frightening shows so that I could listen to them
later in the day.

Now I was having some health challenges when I arrived
at their place, and over a period of the next couple of months

I felt my energy level going down and down. My physical discomfort was getting worse by the day.

Finally, one morning I asked my inner guidance what was going on, and the answer I received was very helpful. I was told that the next time the husband approached me with the latest disaster rumors to tell him, "My friend, I know that you mean well for me, but I have to ask you to hold off on these scary stories of yours. You see, *it's my job to stay uplifted*, no matter what. Your stories are enticing; however, they tend to bring my energy level down. I need to stay up if I'm going to do the work that I came here to do." To make a long story short, he began to honor my request right away, and in a very short time my health and energy level shot back up to normal.

And that's the message for all of us who truly care about the well-being of humanity. It's like a résumé for us, so that when anyone asks us what our job is we can say, "It's my job to stay uplifted, regardless of all the crazy things that are going on around me. In fact, I've come to understand that if everyone buys into the disaster mindset and nobody guards their energy level, then we will all be down wallowing in the swamplands. Some of us have to stay uplifted, and that's what I'm here to do!"

> ### MY INTENTION FOR TODAY IS:
> ●
> *I Intend that I am staying uplifted and doing*
> *what I came here to do.*

DOUBTS
● ● ● ● ● ● ● ● ● ● ● ● ●

How much greater we are than we think we are.

There are three main things that can interfere with the manifestation of our intentions. The first is the "yet" factor, which calls on us to remember that just because something hasn't manifested yet doesn't mean that it's not going to manifest. The second is the Highest Good factor, which asks us to understand that the Universe knows better for us than we know for ourselves. Sometimes it's just not in our Highest Good or the Highest Good of others involved for our intention to manifest. And the third thing that can sabotage us is doubt.

There is an old story about the Knower and the Novice that best explains how to deal with our doubts. When the Novice makes an intention and then, soon after, is faced with doubt or resistance, he tends to buy into the doubts. These doubts can be thoughts coming from inside him that tell him that he can't have, or doesn't deserve, or can't afford whatever it is that he's intended to manifest. Similarly, these doubts can also come from his outside environment in the form of well-meaning friends or business advisors who say that he couldn't possibly manifest his desires. As the Novice buys into the doubts, regardless of their source, he sabotages his experience, loses trust in the Laws of Manifestation, and stops his forward movement.

The Knower is a different story. When the Knower is confronted with doubts or resistances, instead of believing in them, he ignores them and continues moving forward. He understands that the Intention Process always works—that we are all grand Creators, capable of great things—and all we have to do is trust that when we hold onto a thought it will manifest for us. We may not know when or where. We just know that it will.

MY INTENTION FOR TODAY IS:

*I Intend that I am ignoring any doubts
and that I am continuing to move forward
toward the manifestation of my intentions.*

BALANCE

. . . .

If calamity befalls us, we're ready, without complaint.
This is the posture that strengthens our immune system.

As our world goes through its changes leading us to a golden age of manifestation, you will see many people around you who are having a difficult time adapting. During this time of letting go, our values will shift. The homeless and those who have had the least in our culture will surface to be the ones who are the teachers, for they will have already gotten used to being without the fancy things of life.

Conversely, those who have been living off the fat of the land will be the most challenging to be around, and you will see them complaining loudly because they aren't getting all of the things they've become accustomed to having. How you act or react to these people is up to you; however, your best tack is to remain calm and centered regardless of what is going on around you. In this way, you not only set a good example for your troubled brothers and sisters, you also enjoy an added benefit: you'll be healthier. For it is a great truth that those who complain are more apt to attract physical challenges to themselves, while those who can hold their emotional balance in times of change are strengthened.

MY INTENTION FOR TODAY IS:

*I Intend that I am calm regardless
of what is going on around me.*

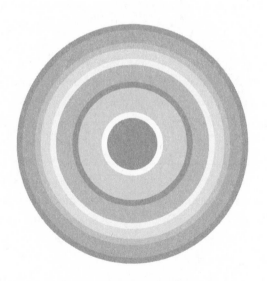

chapter ten

LETTING GO

GROWING UP

The world you live in is splitting apart.
The old selfish ways are collapsing, and,
at the same time,
the new spiritual ways are emerging,
heralding a better life for all.

REMEMBER WHEN YOU WERE A CHILD AND everything was bright and new? As you began to explore your world you looked around at all of the adults and wondered why they acted like they did. They did so many strange things that were making them unhappy.

Later on, as you grew in size and age, choices about what is real and what isn't presented themselves to you, and you told yourself that, for a time, you would play with certain illusions. You knew down deep in your heart that many of the things you believed in were not the truth, but you came to be enamored with them anyway. They made life in society easier for you because everyone else also believed in the same illusions—

illusions about the nature of *ownership, time, what groups you identify with, who you really are,* and so forth. These were the things that were so clear to you when you were a child. You knew they were untrue, but you decided that someday you would set these games and illusions aside when they were no longer useful to you.

The interesting point is that when the time came to discard these games or illusions as no longer useful, we found ourselves continuing to use them anyway. We didn't seem to be able to stop using them. Oh, sometimes we'd catch ourselves and we'd know that what we just said or did wasn't true, but nobody else seemed to notice, and life just went on and the years went by. There would be moments when we were sure that it was time to put all of these illusions away and return to the truth and innocence we knew so well when we were young. These moments began to come closer and closer together and we ran into others who were also talking about putting aside these same illusions that no longer served them.

And now, we're beginning to realize that our whole life must come into its integrity if we are to evolve and be happy. Our whole being cries out for truth. We catch ourselves every time we speak falsely or argue on behalf of our illusions and we pay a high price to continue as we have done for years. Those who require us to uphold our illusions in order to remain agreeable and friendly are clearly not on the same path as us. We intend freedom. We intend peace. We intend our environment clean and beautiful. And we intend true happiness—the happiness we knew as a child.

> ### MY INTENTION FOR TODAY IS:
> . . . .
> *I Intend that I am letting go of any beliefs and values that aren't serving me anymore.*

ILLUSIONS
. . . .

The longer you hold on to the old ways,
when one profits at the expense of another,
the longer your challenges will continue.
However, as soon as you let go
and allow Great Spirit to bring about a solution
that is best for everyone, your challenges will lessen.

It's difficult for some of us to see that our worldly beliefs are temporary, illusionary. We think that it's all written in stone and since everything has been this way for ages, then it must be true and good. After all, if everybody agrees that an hour only has sixty segments, an item just bought at the store really belongs to us, the TV always tells us the truth, our leaders are kind and beneficent, then they must be right, right?

Well, times are changing fast and many of our long-held beliefs and institutions are falling apart before our very eyes. As we step forth into the future, we are seeing that many of the ideas we invested a lifetime in are no longer working for us like they used to. Indeed, if we are going to build a better world for ourselves and for our children, we must begin to reexamine our thinking patterns and be willing to make changes when we run across a belief that's out of date.

Perhaps one of the most illusory of our beliefs centers on who we are. We've been led to believe that we are a name and a body, with all its inherent proclivities and preferences, but this point of view is fast becoming obsolete. Clearly, the hallmark of the age we're stepping into bids us to become more than we thought we were. Let's return to my novel, *The Reunion: A Parable for Peace*, and look closer at this idea.

"Who are you?"

I looked up. No one was in sight. I was alone.

"Who are you?" the invisible voice asked again.

"Robert," I answered sharply. "I'm Robert McCoy."

"Are you sure about that?"

"What?" This was maddening.

"I said, are you sure? Are you sure that you're Robert

McCoy?"

"Yes, I'm Robert McCoy!" I yelled it up at the sky.

"What is it that makes you so sure you're Robert McCoy? Couldn't you just as easily be William Smith or Joe Adams? Isn't Robert McCoy just a name your parents made up?"

"Well, yes. I suppose so," I said. "But that's my name."

Silence. Then, "Are you your name, Robert? Or could it be that you are more than that?"

I didn't know what to say. Up until this point, I'd been mildly annoyed. But now I was beginning to get angry. "Who are you?" I demanded.

Nothing. Not a sound. I stood there surrounded by nothing but the trees and the sky.

"Who are you?" I asked again.

"That's not the question, my brother. The question is who are you? You keep telling me that you are your name, Robert McCoy. But I believe that you're more than that. I believe you're more than a couple of words that come out of your mouth."

"Okay!" I shouted. "I'm Robert McCoy, and I am the body that stands here in front of you!"

"Really?" The voice sounded mildly amused.

"Yes, I am my body."

"And I suppose you're sure about that, too?"

"Yes!" I screamed.

Silence again. Then, finally, "Then you must be your hands. Is that right, Robert. Are you your hands?"

I thought about that for a moment. "No," I answered.

"You sound a little tentative, my brother. Like you're not so sure. Are you your feet then? Answer me that."

This was ridiculous! "No!" I stated. "I'm definitely more than my hands and my feet!"

"Good for you, Robert," came the voice. "Because what I'm suggesting to you is that you are much more than your name, much more than your hands and feet, and much more than your body, as well."

It's hard to explain what happened next. A feeling of great melancholy swept over me. I was totally disoriented; my legs gave way underneath me, as I crumpled to the ground and began sobbing. Tears flowed until none were left. Somewhere in the middle of it all, as I lay whimpering face down on a bed of soft pine needles, a new sensation—I don't even know if it was a thought or a feeling—came to me. Yes! I am more than my body! I am a Being who lives inside of my body!

And with this revelation, two things happened at once: the shift in my perceptions that I'd experienced yesterday came back. The stones and trees and leaves and everything around me came alive and shimmered even brighter than before. At the same time, a strange and beautiful man appeared...

MY INTENTION FOR TODAY IS:
. . . .

I Intend that I am taking a closer look
at my core beliefs about myself
and the world I live in.

WINDOW-SHOPPING
. . . .

When we realize that we are becoming
exactly like those we oppose, shouldn't that be reason enough
for us to stop opposing them?

As we undergo this transformative process, we talk a lot about the old ways and the new ways of doing things. The current world acceleration requires us to adapt to challenges and situations that may be uncomfortable at first, but, with a shift in our perspective, all things come into focus. We see that the new ways are actually beneficial for us; that they offer the promise of something far grander than the current mainstream matrix. In order to slip gracefully into the new paradigm we only need to let go.

I've always enjoyed window-shopping. You know what window-shopping is: it's going out to the stores with no intention of buying anything. When I window-shop, I tell myself that, today, I'm leaving my wallet in my pocket. I'm just going to look in the windows, no matter how tempting the shop owners present their wares.

I treat our current way of life the same way. I'm only window-shopping it. I'm not buying anything anymore. When the media, for instance, tells me that there is some new problem out there, and the solution is now being made available to everyone, I simply observe it. My experience has taught me, time and time again, that the media is self-serving, and they have no interest whatsoever in my well-being. In fact, it's just the opposite—the media creates problems for us in order to get us to buy ideas and consumer goods.

In the old days, I would have gotten angry and begun to oppose their media gyrations, thus dissipating my precious energy. But now that I've started to integrate The Code into my life, I've come to understand that I am becoming just like whomever or whatever I am opposing.

So now I window-shop. I observe only, with no emotional attachment to the ideas they're selling on TV and in the newspapers. I'm not buying any of it, so I'm no longer feeding it, and I'm no longer becoming like those I used to oppose. This is one of the keys to our ultimate happiness. We let go by becoming observers.

Those who are living in their highest light know that it is good to share your life and your love, for we have, indeed, come together for a reason. Feel free to fill your days and nights with love for your partner, your family, your friends, your pets, your possessions and everything, for these are all gifts unto you. Just remember that it is unwise to let your attachment to anyone or anything take one minute away from your joy.

> **MY INTENTION FOR TODAY IS:**
>
> *I Intend that I am observing the world around me and, in this way, I am doing my part to usher in a golden age of manifestation.*

THE OLD WAYS AND THE NEW WAYS

The Native American teachers are returning.
They speak to you through your reading
and in the stillness of your mind.
Sometimes they even speak to you
through the rocks, the animals, the trees, or the wind.

Here is a short story to introduce you to the old ways and the new ways:

While living in New Mexico, I found that I liked going out into the desert, and it was there, on a mesa near Chaco Canyon, where I made an intention to access higher knowledge. I went into a mild trance, and suddenly Kokopelli, the most outrageous being I ever met, appeared. After playing his flute and dancing around for a while, he told me that one of humanity's most fascinating traits had to do with our strange but stubborn urge to hold onto beliefs and activities that didn't serve us anymore. He placed our current collective reality in that category and made light of it, saying that these characteristics were soon to be obsolete and seen by the masses as the old ways (not to be confused with the ways of our ancient ancestors when they were in their glory). He pointed out that the abbreviation for the old ways is "OW!" and he got up and jumped around like he'd just stubbed his toe. We laughed for a long time, and then he went on to say that the new evolved ways, as represented in The Code, were abbreviated "NEW!" and that they would lead us out of our current despair into a golden age.

"Take your pick!" he said, as he hopped around on one leg, "OW or NEW!" and each time he shouted "OW!" he exaggerated his pain even more. I'll never forget how hard we laughed. Later on, when I was confronted by a difficult situation that stemmed from me holding on too tightly to my old ways, it was somehow easier to deal with if I recalled his antics that day out on the mesa.

MY INTENTION FOR TODAY IS:

I Intend that I am taking time to play and have a lot of fun.

INTEGRATING

For every point of view, its opposite is equally valid.

How often do we scoff at another person's idea, thinking that there is no way it could possibly work? Instead of giving them the benefit of the doubt, we go on our merry way, judging and telling ourselves how wrong they are. What we don't see, however, is the effect that this line of behavior is having on us. In isolating our thought processes we shut out a potential avenue or approach that we may want to explore later.

It's interesting, too, how the Universe has ways of helping us integrate all sides of an issue. Just when we least expect it, we can find ourselves in a situation where everything we scoffed at earlier now makes the greatest of sense.

When one is trusting in the innate goodness of the Universe, it's easy to give up our old ways of doing things. Our reliance upon everything from poor leadership to destructive energy sources melts away in the light of new, more pleasing alternatives. There are those, of course, who will cry out that the transition will be too rough; that if they were to let go of their present way of life, there wouldn't be enough food on the table or there wouldn't be a roof over their heads. In short, they're unable to envision a way to step into the new paradigm that doesn't threaten their current security and survival belief systems.

To these people, our response is always the same: Seek self-empowerment. You can have complete control over your life. Others cannot dictate your reality to you unless you let them. By your thoughts, you create your world. And you can choose to change it all.

> **MY INTENTION FOR TODAY IS:**
> . . . .
> *I Intend that I am accepting and integrating*
> *all points of view.*

TREASURE HUNTING
. . . .

Keep asking—keep opening—keep finding.
Make it a quest.

What could be more fun than heading out on a quest for hidden treasure? A treasure hunt offers the excitement of going to exotic places, sharing mystical experiences, and the promise of riches and glory. Every one of us has a searcher inside who, at one time or another, longs to take part in a magical journey which calls upon us to summon our heartiest courage, overcome seemingly insurmountable obstacles, venture blindly into the darkest of caverns, and dig deep for rewards that we aren't even sure are there.

Oftentimes, the only guide we may have is an old, worn-out, dog-eared map or ancient manuscript left to us by a previous treasure hunter who was generally considered to be a bit eccentric. Our closest friends and advisors think that we are foolish, but still we are lured on by forces that we don't even fully comprehend.

Such is the predilection of the treasure seeker who discards all warnings, leaves everything behind, and sets out on a search for long-lost gold and jewels, the value of which defies the imagination.

Everyday life, however, does not often grace the average man or woman with the opportunity to sojourn to foreign lands in search of buried riches. Everyday life keeps our days filled with repetitive goings, doings, and distractions. We must seek elsewhere for hidden treasures.

Fortunately for us, there is a mystical place, vastly unexplored, which is within our reach. We need not travel farther than our favorite armchair. As we sit quietly and gaze into the cavernous darkness behind our closed eyes, a glittering backdrop comes into view and beckons us to explore further. A distant speck of light appears and pulls us toward it as we let go and allow ourselves to be pulled. Obstacles in the form of random thoughts demand our attention and threaten to interfere with our quest. But, as we persevere and hold our concentration upon the light, a new realm opens up before us. We find ourselves in a place where the potentiality of our experience expands far beyond the scope of our everyday awareness—indeed far beyond we'd ever thought possible.

There, inside the comforting white light, we uncover riches much more priceless than any Earthly treasure. So much so that if we possessed a giant chest full of the world's rarest gems, or a vault full of gold worth millions and millions of dollars, we would gladly trade it all for a single moment spent delighting in the glorious treasure we have found within.

MY INTENTION FOR TODAY IS:

I Intend that I am treasure hunting within daily.

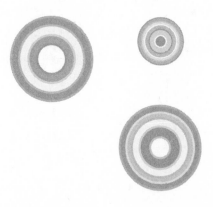

chapter eleven

FREEDOM

FREEDOM

*Start with yourself and then move out into the world
and the world will welcome you with open arms.*

EACH OF US IS LIKE A CELL IN AN IMMENSE ENTITY
called humanity. When we all work together synergistically,
then all is well and we are capable of great things. When we
work separately or against each other, humanity as a whole
as well as each one of us suffers. Isn't it time, now, for us to
do what we came here to do in earnest? Let us realize, as The
Code says, that miracles are bestowed as we hold our attention
on that which connects us and discard that which separates us.

The world nowadays needs more warriors for peace; people
who realize that solutions sought on the battlefield will not
provide results that work on our behalf. The true battlefield
does not stretch out across blood-drenched soils or campus

lawns, but is in our own hearts and minds. When enough people begin to put away all patriotic thoughts and envision our world in its highest light, then we will, at long last, be at peace.

It starts out with a few courageous souls who declare themselves free, and who are willing to live that ideal for all the world to see. Then a few more will glean the wisdom of being their own sovereign authority. Not long after that, a larger mass will find their inner balance and reclaim that which belongs to them. And finally, our entire worldview shifts as all human beings who walk this Earth stand united as one, dedicated to allowing people everywhere to live their lives in absolute freedom. That is the key to realizing our highest potential and we must hold onto it and pamper it as if it is the greatest gift in our possession.

We are blossoming in all our glory. Peace, freedom, creativity, abundance, and joy for all are ours for the intending. Worlds within worlds reveal themselves as atom and galaxy alike welcome us and bid us to explore to our heart's content. All that and more await, but first we must do one more thing before we set out for new horizons.

We must begin to join together in small groups, and then use our collective imagination to connect these groups to one another. When enough of us are embracing the vision of all groups everywhere, merging our lights and coming together as one, we will reawaken to that which we have already known—that this feeling of Oneness is our home, our place of comfort where we find our true selves and take a breather before embarking upon other exciting adventures out there in the endless, eternal Universe.

MY INTENTION FOR TODAY IS:

*I Intend that I am clearly shown
my next step in life.*

EXPANDING

Think bigger, better, more...

There are no limits. All of our limits are self-imposed even though it may often appear otherwise. What we overlook is that we make the final decision about whether we buy into a limiting belief or not. Others may try to suggest or persuade us that it is in our best interests to harbor a particular belief, but most often it's only in the best interests of the person who is doing the persuading. They'd feel a lot better if we would do things the way everybody else is doing them.

Perhaps, at this point, it would be a good idea to take a closer look at our collective reality and see how it got to be the way it is. When we were young children, we looked to those who were bigger than us to instruct us in the ways of life, and, because we were innocent, we trusted them to start us off on the right foot. In most cases they taught us as best they could, but only in rare instances did they teach us anything that was outside the standard, agreed-upon, status quo reality. In accordance with human nature, we merged our beliefs with theirs and began to go along with the crowd.

As the years went by and we matured, we found that it was easiest for us to stay with the set of ideas we originally learned because these ideas were supported by almost everyone else around us. It seldom occurred to us to deviate from the main-stream, and yet, for a few people, a subtle voice inside whis-pered that they did not need to be supported by others in their thinking processes. These insightful people realized that they were free to believe as they chose, even if others didn't approve.

So, how about breaking out of the pack? We don't need the approval of others to think—and create—what we like. We can think "bigger" and enhance our opportunities immensely; we can think "better" and improve the quality of our lives beyond measure; we can think "more" and increase the flow of all good things coming to us. And we can start right now by taking a closer look at all of our limiting ideas and tossing them in the garbage with all the other things that we don't need anymore.

MY INTENTION FOR TODAY IS:

I Intend that I am thinking bigger, better, more...

FREEING OUR SPIRIT

How do you nurture the growing light?
You keep believing it will continue to grow.

Before we can have true freedom we have to be able to learn from our experiences. This means that we stop repeating the same behavior that has been causing us discomfort, and instead, change our attitudes and actions. This is how we achieve a different result, one that serves us and every one around us better.

As our light seeks for its fullest radiance we will gradually slide out from under the shadows of others who would continue to control us as long as we let them, and step into our own sovereign power, independent and strong in the knowledge that each and every one of us is free to create to our heart's content, that we are helped every step of the way, and that nothing can stop us unless we allow it.

We can have it all. But first we must be ready to make some changes in our lives.

For the past two years I've taken daily walks around the lake near where I live. It's my favorite form of exercise and, at the same time, the magnificent vistas of the surrounding mountains provide me with a perfect environment for opening up to new creative ideas.

As is my custom, I walk steadily, never stopping along the way except to take occasional notes and to pet a friendly, reddish-brown dog who guards a house by the lake. I call him Rusty, although I doubt that that's what his owners named him. He's a part collie, part chow cross, and he's chained alone to a small doghouse that sits away from the owner's house, out in the middle of the yard. Snow, rain or shine, day in and day out, one thing never changed on my walks: Rusty was always there.

When I first moved into the neighborhood Rusty was younger, and he would bark and jump and run wildly toward me until the chain jerked him to a sudden halt. That didn't stop him though. Back then, Rusty was lively and full of Spirit. But over the last couple of years something inside him shifted. Now, he's no longer as lively. It's as if he's been beaten down by the boredom and he's resigned himself to living his days at the end of a chain. His Spirit only comes to life in the evening when, for a brief moment, his owner delivers a bowl of food and a few pats on the head before going back into the house.

One day about four months ago, something interesting happened. Just before sunset on a chilly spring evening, I was walking by in my usual way, admiring the last of the season's snow that still whitened the peaks in the distance, when Rusty's owner came out with his nightly bowl of food. Rusty jumped up and ran to the length of the chain, only this time, instead of jerking him back into place, it broke.

I watched from a distance as Rusty pranced and danced like never before, free as a bird! At first he stayed well out of the range of his owner who called and cajoled him for several minutes, all the while cussing the chilly wind and the situation in general. He just wanted to get the dog fed and get back into his toasty, warm house.

Rusty, on the other hand, ran and played around like a young pup, enjoying his first feeling of freedom in years. His eyes, usually so sullen and sad, sparkled now, with a newfound brightness. His Spirit was returning; he had come back to life, and I whispered a silent prayer that he would run away and take his chances out in the world. You see, I'm always trusting that the Universe takes care of us, as long as we intend it for ourselves. To me it looked like anything would be better than going back to living on a chain.

It was starting to get darker, and as I rounded the end of the lake and turned back toward home, I watched as the owner went back into the house and came out a minute later holding a bag of special treats high in the air and shaking them loudly. Within moments Rusty was back on the chain. He was unable to resist the temptation of the tasty nuggets.

The following day Rusty was there as usual. The sparkle was gone as he lay there in the dirt with those sad, expressive eyes. Attached to his collar was a new chain, shorter and stronger than the first. He looked horrible, but at the same time there was something different in him, like he hadn't completely forgotten how good it felt to be free the day before. I went up to give him a rub behind the ears, and I was talking to him like I talk to all the animals (Hi guy! How's it going, etc.?), only this time my curiosity got the best of me and I asked him why he gave up his freedom to live his life chained in the yard, just for the sake of a few treats?

In an instant, his Spirit, which seemed so faraway only moments before, lit up, and his answer shot telepathically through my mind. He said, "Hey Tony, no one's home yet.

How about if you undo this heavy chain and we'll see if I fall for that same old trick again?"

I'd better not tell you what I did.

MY INTENTION FOR TODAY IS:

· ·

*I Intend that I am learning from my experiences
so that I am only repeating the ones
that bring me happiness.*

GLOBAL OBSERVANCE DAY

· ·

You are learning the language that has no words.

As a way of celebrating the success of our transformative processes, we'd like to propose a new holiday: Global Observance Day. And what historical event or remembrance, you may ask, are we observing? The answer is none whatsoever. This is not about creating a new event on our calendars so that we need to buy or sell more greeting cards, or glorify labor unions, or honor a "discoverer" who coldly massacred entire tribes of peaceful natives, or rouse more patriotism so our friendly arms and airplane manufacturers can make more money. No, this is something different entirely. It's a truly challenging, invigorating experience, designed to have us look at the world around us in a new way. Here's how it works:

Pick a day—any day you like—and for as long as you can remember to do so, simply observe what goes on around you (hence the name Global Observance Day). On this day, you're not going to judge, label, categorize, analyze, record, or even give a name to anything in your immediate world. Likewise, you needn't believe, accept, reject, or react to anyone else's ideas unless you want to. All you have to do is witness what's going on.

Other than that, you can go happily about your day as usual. If you drive somewhere, you can be observing while you're driving. If you go to work, you can still be just as efficient (perhaps even more so) by refraining from making any judgments. If you choose to interact with others during this time, you can tell them what you are doing or not; it doesn't matter. Those who are concerned about how people might react, or who feel that it would be easier to stay in an "observing mode" if there were less distractions around them, may want to spend the day out in nature, taking a walk, or sitting beside the lake. It's up to you.

After you get good at impartially observing your outer, worldly surroundings, then go on to observing your inner thoughts without judging them. If you notice at any time throughout the day that you've slipped back into judging or labeling things, be easy on yourself. Don't browbeat yourself; simply start over with your impartial observing. Even if you have to begin anew a hundred times over the course of the day, that's okay. Eventually your perceptions will shift and when you least expect it, you will step into a world that was unavailable to you when you were putting your spin on everything. You'll get a glimpse of the world as it really is, where everything is connected to everything else, where everything glows, and where you know you are part and parcel of a Great Oneness that has been there all along. From that point on, you'll be less apt to harm or judge anyone ever again because you'll know that you would only be harming or judging another part of yourself.

> No wrong, no right
> No dark, no light
> No good, no bad
> No sane, no mad.
> No low, no high
> No yours, no my
> No rich, no poor
> No less, no more.
> No weak, no strong
> No short, no long
> No big, no small

No spin at all.
No there, no here
No far, no near
No gain, no name
It's all the same.
It just is.

MY INTENTION FOR TODAY IS:

*I Intend that I am observing
my surroundings impartially.*

chapter twelve

HEALING

WELLNESS

*It is for yourself that you see
others in their highest light.*

NO ONE IS WELL SERVED BY ANOTHER WHO, EITHER consciously or unconsciously, talks about disease. The best thing that you can do for anyone is to hold the light for them, seeing them in their perfect state of wellness. Regardless of what they tell you about their maladies, you do them no favor by agreeing with them about their illnesses. When they are temporarily unable to hold the light for themselves, you can hold it for them. You help them by holding a vision in your mind of them in their highest light. And, in this way, you are not reinforcing their sickness and suffering. You are reinforcing their wellness.

When we first started the Intenders, it was common to hear someone putting their sick friends or family into the circle. We would talk about someone's disease, and then intend that it is healed. This practice went on for quite a while, but we didn't seem to be getting the results we desired from it. So, one evening, we decided to ask our guides and helpers about this. The answer we received was very profound.

We were told that when we give a name to somebody's sickness that we are giving power unto it. We were reminded that our words have power, and when we speak the name of any disease—whether we think it is our own or someone else's—we are actually reinforcing or feeding the disease. This does not help us if our highest priority is to preserve and perpetuate our lives.

We were also reminded that our thoughts are things, and that we are all transmitters and receivers of thoughts. On a level that is normally invisible to us, these thoughts fly through space, just like radio or TV waves, and they are received by the person we are thinking about. When we send out a thought that pictures someone else in it, this thought is received and it tends to manifest. We are all constantly making suggestions with our thoughts to others of how we would like them to be.

So, when we envision others as suffering in any way, we are

contributing to their suffering. Conversely, when we see them in their highest light—happy and full of vitality—that is the message they receive. And that is the message that will help them the most.

> **MY INTENTION FOR TODAY IS:**
> . . . .
> *I Intend that I am seeing everyone,*
> *including myself, in their highest light—*
> *happy, healthy, whole, and humming.*

CONFIRMATION

. . . .

Prayer and fasting heal just about anything
in a few short days.

It's a strange predilection of mankind that we look for confirmation for our aliments. We look to see what happened to everybody else who has experienced similar symptoms to ours, and, in doing so, we do ourselves a great disservice. What many people don't realize is that just because somebody else developed a chronic condition after showing similar symptoms to ours doesn't mean that we will do the same.

We are all dealing with toxic thoughts, substances, and experiences in our world that may or may not present us with short-term aches, pains, bumps, zits, and so forth. It's a part of life nowadays. What we oftentimes forget is that a great many of the things we think we have "wrong" with us are only temporary. They'll go away by themselves in a short time if we leave them alone. Oh sure, sometimes we'll need to adjust our diet or our work habits for a while, and that is natural.

But it's unnatural for us to look too deeply for confirmation for the causes for our ailments. In fact, we put ourselves in harm's way when we delve too deeply, parading every disease imaginable before us, in our quest to find out the cause of an ache or pain. We tend to make things chronic that would have only been temporary.

You see people do this all the time. They'll get a new bump somewhere on their body and begin to mull over all the reasons as to how it could possibly have gotten there. They'll check out magazines, talk to friends, and have doctors run test after test as they search frantically to find out what happened to others who also had similar bumps. In order to validate their own theories (which are growing rapidly now), they'll even resort to looking for coincidences. For example, while walking through a popular coffee shop, they might notice a newspaper sitting on a table with an article in it that describes what happened to a person who had a similar bump, and lo and behold, they treat this as a confirmation for their own condition, and thus make it worse.

Fortunately, there are a couple of good antidotes for the toxicity in our world today. First, we can always remind ourselves that we are creating whatever we put our attention on, and that when we dig too deeply in search of explanations for our aches and pains, we run the risk of bringing other possibilities into the picture that have nothing to do with our original situation. Instead, we can tell ourselves that we are fine and that we do not choose to use our bodies to act out any sickness scenarios. According to the Law, as we envision ourselves being happy, healthy, and whole, that is what we will create.

And second, we can trust that whatever is bothering us is only temporary and will go away on its own very soon. The shamans and medicine men of old knew that prayer and fasting healed almost everything in a few days. It could be that instead of spending our precious energy in search of confirmation for what ails us, we could stop eating or begin a Master Cleanse, retire into a quiet place where we can be alone for a while, and ask God to help us.

Please understand that we are not saying there is anything wrong with going to a medical practitioner. If you believe that a doctor will help you, then, by all means, that is the route for you to follow. Likewise, if you have a broken bone or need a cut stitched up, then doctors are the experts and can be of great help. But when it comes to diagnosing sicknesses, it's a guessing game and we are still in the medical dark ages. It's easy to come out of a hospital or doctor's office nowadays feeling worse than when you went in. On the other hand, if you can bring yourself to believe in it, you have just as good or a better chance of getting rid of your health challenges through prayer and fasting than by all the remedies prescribed by the credentialed medical establishment. That's a universal fact.

> **MY INTENTION FOR TODAY IS:**
> . . . .
> *I Intend that I am purifying my body*
> *every so often through prayer and fasting.*

LUMPING
. . . .

Agreement is the glue that holds realities together.

Lumping is a term we use to describe when we decide we're going to be like everyone else. We "lump ourselves in" with a collective of people who are all appearing to have the same thing going on in their lives.

As an example let's say that the crowd believes that gaining weight happens as a result of our eating (instead of our thinking) habits. If we agree with them, then we'll surely be concerned with every little thing we eat and therefore set ourselves up for getting fat.

It works the same with diseases. If, for instance, we agree that a particular disease, *the Black Crud*, is running rampant throughout the population, then we run the risk of getting it. Our agreement with everyone else who believes in it creates an opening for us to experience it. If, however, a well-meaning friend warns us that *the Black Crud* is spreading, and we choose to withhold our agreement and our belief in it, then we will not be subjected to it.

It's at the moment that we lend our agreement to a belief that we bring it to life.

Perhaps it would be a good idea for us to take a closer look at that subtle "moment of agreement" which is so important in our lives. Let's say we're riding on a ferry and the nice lady sitting next to us points to a young man across the aisle and remarks that he doesn't look well. Casually, she elaborates, "I hope he doesn't have that nasty *Black Crud* that's going around. I saw a blurb on the news last night that said that ferries, buses, and airplanes are 'likely places' where you could easily catch it."

Now the ball is in our court. If we agree with the nice lady, either by saying "Yes" or even by simply nodding our head in the slightest degree, we have just set the wheels in motion for all sorts of ugly things to manifest. First, we've sent a mental, telepathic message to the young man across the aisle reinforcing his ill health—not a very loving thing to do. Second, if we happen to believe in the illusion of contagion or "germ theory," then we create a scenario whereby we could "catch" the disease. And finally, if we agree that ferries are "likely places" for germs to spread, then we reinforce the likelihood of our getting sick. Remember, it is we who create our reality, not somebody else—*unless we give them our agreement.*

This all becomes clearer when we begin to see that with each decision to agree we dig ourselves deeper into a hole. From a higher perspective, however, each and every one of us is a unique Being, and whatever imbalance we're experiencing at any given time, whether it is a slight pain or a persistent ailment, is unique unto us. We had different parents than everyone else, different schooling, different genetics, different experiences entirely. But when we lump ourselves in with everyone else who is having similar symptoms by agreeing with the doctor, or the newscaster, or the nice lady on the ferry that we have or could get *the Black Crud*, we do ourselves a tremendous disservice and we set the stage for us to have to live out the manifestation of our beliefs.

You see, our mind is much more active and astute than we give it credit for. It knows the symptoms of every disease out there. In fact, just by hearing the name of any disease, the mind will send its messages to the body to begin replicating the symptoms associated with it.

That's the way diseases are created. The important thing

to remember is that *we don't have what they had,* and it is our choice to either agree with others or we can see ourselves in our highest light, perfect, happy, and whole. Indeed, we are grand creators who might want to consider becoming much more careful about what we agree upon, lest we create it.

MY INTENTION FOR TODAY IS:

*I Intend that I am watching my thoughts
much closer and I am remembering
that my agreement is a precious tool
only to be used after careful consideration.*

SHINING LIGHT AND SENDING LOVE

Allow healing to occur no matter where it comes from.

In working with the laws of manifestation, we have talked many times about seeing the end result from the beginning, and nowhere is that act more important than in healing our fellow travelers. When we see them in their highest light, we are, in fact, holding a vision of them already healed. This, along with invoking the Love of God, is the first principle of true healing. It is the way the Masters did it, but now many are learning this process today, even some of our indigo teenagers like Bonnie in the story below.

"I don't know," Ruby Jean cautioned. "You'd have to be very careful. It's awfully hard to tell how strong some of those branches are."

"Yeah," Bonnie echoed. "You'd have to be very careful. Maybe you'd better not."

"It's not so high. I'll bet I could get some nuts for us to eat," Jenny persisted, disregarding the warnings of the other two. Then she began to shinny up the trunk to the first branches. "Look, it's not so hard!" As Bonnie and Ruby Jean looked up, a few leaves fell off of the branches down onto their faces.

"Jenny, be careful!" R. J. pleaded again, but Jenny climbed even higher.

"It's no problem. I see a hole up here that I can get to in just a minute." Jenny stepped up onto a smaller branch and suddenly the branch gave way with a sharp cracking sound.

Jenny gave a surprised cry and grabbed at the lower branches as she fell, but she couldn't hold on. In an instant, she was on the ground, screaming in pain. Her left leg just below her knee was bent at a forty-five degree angle. An ugly damp red spot of blood began slowly saturating the leg of her jeans.

"Oh no! Jenny, are you okay?" Bonnie and Ruby Jean cried out as they ran to her. "Are you okay? What can we do? What do we do now?"

"You run for help, and I'll stay here with Jenny." Bonnie fought to stay calm.

"Okay," Ruby Jean agreed, and she immediately sprinted off in the direction of her home.

What happened next wasn't witnessed by anyone, other than the two squirrels up in the hickory tree. Ten-year-old Bonnie Moore had never been in a situation like this before. She didn't know what to do but she knew she had to do something. Jenny was lying there shaking and screaming and bleeding.

Bonnie knelt down and told Jenny that everything was going to be all right. She brushed Jenny's hair off her forehead and the fear and pain she saw in her friend's eyes tugged at her heart and made her want to cry. She could see that Jenny was getting paler and shaking harder with each passing moment and, more than anything, Bonnie wanted to help her. She could hear her father and mother telling her that she could do anything her heart believed in. She remembered a time when one of her dad's friends had gotten hurt. Her parents had been talking about his friend's healing and her dad had said, "You can help people heal by seeing them in their highest light. That's how the Master did it. He first envisioned them as well and whole so they could heal." And in that moment, Bonnie knew exactly what to do.

A serenity that she had never felt before came over her as she looked down at Jenny and, in her mind, she saw Jenny's leg as good as new. She rubbed her hands together and ever so slowly and delicately, she began to pet the broken leg. Stoking gently, calmly back and forth from the knee to the ankle, sometimes not even actually touching the leg. She began to speak. "Holy Father Mother God, I ask for light and love. I am shining light and sending love." She kept repeating these words over and over, continuing all the while to stroke the wound ever so lightly. "Shining light and sending love, shining light and sending love." Bonnie Moore knew that something good, something wonderful, was happening. It felt like a warm light was filling her body and directing itself through her heart and her hands into Jenny's mangled leg. Jenny's sobs subsided to whimpers as the pain abated and the warmth spread through her. She closed her eyes and, with a deep sigh, surrendered to her healing.

"Shining light and sending love, shining light and sending love." Bonnie wasn't sure how long she had been petting Jenny's leg when, unexpectedly, she heard a "snap." Jenny groaned, and the leg slowly began to move. The bleeding stopped and, as if by some unseen force, the leg continued to straighten. With a calmness belying her years, Bonnie kept chanting, "Shining light and sending love. Thank you Holy Mother Father God," as she continued petting and stroking gently.

Another snapping sound and all of a sudden Jenny's leg

looked like it had returned to its normal position. Bonnie stopped stroking when Jenny suddenly sat up and reached to hug her. A few moments later, they pulled away from each other, and Jenny dryly said, "I hate nuts anyway," sending both girls into uncontrollable giggles.

Ten more minutes went by and cries were heard from the distance. "Where is she? Oh my God, where is she?" Running frantically, Jenny's mother and father, Rob and Liz Eastman, and Ruby Jean appeared from around the bend in the trail, only to find Jenny and Bonnie standing there, hugging each other and laughing.

"Jenny, my baby, are you all right?" screamed her mother, seeing the blood on her daughter's pants.

"Sure mom, I'm fine," Jenny responded, as she tried to extricate herself from her mother's tight hug. "Really!"

Everyone was panting heavily, trying to catch their breath and figure out what had happened. Bonnie smiled sweetly at the people there. She had a peaceful look on her face, a glow in her eyes. "Let's go home and get something to drink. I'm thirsty," she said.

The bewildered group didn't say a word. They started walking back down the woodland trail, each cautiously checking Jenny to see if anything was really wrong with her. It was hard to believe that Ruby Jean would make up such a fantastic story about Jenny falling out of a hickory tree. There didn't seem to be anything wrong with Jenny. She didn't even walk with a limp. And yet, there was a large bloodstain running down her pant leg. The three young girls walked hand in hand chattering away as if nothing had happened.

A short time later when they all stepped inside one of the partially completed Intenders barns, a crowd gathered around them. Liz Eastman took her daughter's face in her hands and looked into her eyes. "Ruby Jean, what made you do such a thing? It's not like you to make up something like that. You gave us all a terrible scare."

Everyone was listening. Ruby Jean's confusion was evident; she didn't know what to say.

"Young lady, can you tell us exactly what happened back there?"

All eyes were on Ruby Jean, awaiting a reasonable explanation, but it was Jenny who looked up at Liz and answered.

"Shining light and sending love, Mrs. Eastman," she said with a smile. "When I fell out of the hickory tree and broke my leg, Bonnie fixed it by shining light and sending love."

The Course in Miracles says that we are healed as we let God teach us to heal. Isn't it time that we started practicing, in earnest? Won't it be wonderful when there are a whole bunch of us walking the Earth and healing each other?

> **MY INTENTION FOR TODAY IS:**
>
> *I Intend that I am learning*
> *to heal my fellow travelers.*

BECOMING LESS SUGGESTIBLE

All diseases have been healed.

We do ourselves a great disservice when we believe that we have a particular sickness and call it by name. When we do this we are discounting the fact that each of us is a unique Being who has had different experiences, different parents, different genetics, and so forth that brought us to the state of imbalance we are dealing with. By believing what a doctor or someone else tells us about ourselves we lump ourselves in with everyone else who has ever had similar symptoms to ours, not realizing that our mind, in its infinite wisdom, will begin to send messages to our body, telling it to create the symptoms we are believing in. And, since our thoughts are always creating our experiences, our body will immediately comply with the mind's wishes and begin to manifest the disease we believe we have.

Wouldn't it be better to hold a vision of ourselves in our highest light and manifest that message instead?

Many years ago the Rosicrucians set up experiments to show us the power that our thoughts have upon our body. They hypnotized people and then approached them with a normal pencil or pen, telling them that the pen was a red-hot poker, like a branding iron. Then they touched the pen to the person's arm and guess what? The person would immediately cry out in pain and a blister began to form. Within moments, the arm took on all the physical characteristics of having been burned.

Stories like this have been hidden from us, but their message is clear. We human beings are very suggestible and it serves us well to remember that we are each unique. Likewise, it does not serve us to believe everything everyone else tells us about ourselves. Not only could their suggestions be entirely wrong, but if we also believe them, we run the risk of manifesting all sorts of things we're apt to wish we'd stayed away from.

> **MY INTENTION FOR TODAY IS:**
> . . . .
> *I Intend that I always remember that I am*
> *a unique Being, capable of so much more*
> *than I've been led to believe.*

DEVICES
. . . .

Your thoughts to the contrary can override the good.

Here in the west, we are subjected to advertising almost everywhere we go. The newspapers, magazines, billboards, and especially the TV are constantly bombarding us with products and services designed to cure all our ills. What's most interesting about this is that before we tuned into the media, we may not have had anything wrong with us. In fact, we could have been fit as a fiddle.

But fit as a fiddle doesn't sell products, so the corporate decision-makers have taken it upon themselves to create problems and challenges for us in order to get us to buy their goods. Said another way, the companies behind all the advertising are actively and deliberately doing their best to make us sick so they can turn a profit.

There are worlds where activities that are purposely designed to harm the health and well-being of others are illegal. Those who choose to engage in these nefarious endeavors are exiled. It matters not if the methods used are subliminal, suggestive, or outright deceptive, those who are caught must leave and cannot return again until they have learned to love.

Let's go back, at this point, to the original premise that is the foundation for all the Intenders' teachings: our thoughts create our world. This means that our thoughts are creating our sicknesses, and our thoughts are the tools we use to get well again. The medics and media would have us believe otherwise by telling us that now they have a fantastic new device that will rid us of all our ills, but, as we are learning, it's the thought of wellness—seeing ourselves healthy and in our highest light— that overrides the need for any device. If, however, we believe that a device—which could be anything from a pill, to a scientific looking apparatus, to a common quartz crystal—is what we need to heal ourselves, then that is the route we should take, because that is what we believe will work. Conversely, if we do not believe that a particular device will work, then we are wasting our time to go any further with it.

When the smokescreen settles and all truths are revealed, we will see that it is the belief that heals us, not the device. You can have a closet full of devices, and if you do not believe a hundred percent in any of them, they won't do you enough good to make any difference. The only device that is capable of curing all of our ills is not to be purchased at your local drugstore or ordered through some obscure catalog. It is not to be found by handing your power and authority over to anyone else, no matter how persuasive or credentialed they may be.

Indeed, the human mind is the greatest device in existence, and all we have to do to make it work on our behalf is learn how to use it.

MY INTENTION FOR TODAY IS:

*I Intend that I am holding my mind
on my desired outcome and trusting implicitly
that it will come to me.*

AGING

*Come from a place of balance—
physical, emotional, mental, and spiritual balance.*

What is it about us that we tend to focus on the problems and limitations of life? If we would focus on that which we'd like to see, we'd be creating it. Aging is a good example of this. As the shift from the old ways to the new ways of living sets in, we find ourselves learning to stretch our thinking processes beyond their old boundaries. Now that we know that our body will physiologically follow the dictates of our mind, we are no longer served by many of our old thinking and speaking habits, especially those surrounding aging and how we talk about it.

Over the course of human history, we have lived long and we have lived short. It wasn't too long ago that the average human life span was under fifty years of age; now it's over eighty, and going up. These figures tell us about our collective tendencies, but they don't explain the anomalies or our potentials.

Remember Methuselah, living for a thousand years? Or St. Germain, who never seemed to age even after being seen decades later by friends who knew him well? Or how about Babaji in India or Thoth in Egypt, both of whom are still supposed to be around, living forever? People have seen these men on too many occasions for us to dismiss their stories lightly. What are they doing that we're not?

To begin with, these long lifers aren't buying into the collective, consensual reality by associating certain physical manifestations with their age. For example, it's doubtful that they believe we tend to lose our memory as we get older; or that when we reach certain milestones, everything slows down for us. No, they're a lot more careful about how they create their future. They don't give voice to their limitations. You'd never hear them say something like, "I think I'm going to need eyeglasses now that I'm getting older," or "the older I get, the harder it gets." Instead, they are marching to a different drummer, one that stays alert and positive in all situations.

Many Masters have taught that once our perceptions enhance and we gain access into the invisible worlds that surround us, we get to the stage where we can literally create the form, shape, and age of our bodies as we so desire. Such is our birthright as Spiritual Beings occupying a human form. Indeed, once we learn to rejuvenate ourselves and create the body of our choosing, they tell us we'll look back at these times and wonder how we could have ever participated in any conversations that limited us so drastically. They say that the glib catchphrases, especially those which describe us as we get older, won't be a part of our vocabularies like they are now.

As we drifted along gently toward the light, my new friend (Kukulcan), elaborated on many of the Earthly illusions. In every case, he said that we have unwittingly identified with our body, believing it to be our true Self, when, in fact, we are the essence within it. As an example, he said that when we believe we are a certain number of years old, we are actually identifying with the age of our body. But, as he explained further, our true essence is eternal and incapable of aging. The only thing we accomplish by identifying with our body's age is to cause it to get older faster than it would have if we hadn't been thinking (or talking) about it.

MY INTENTION FOR TODAY IS:

I Intend that I am beginning to rejuvenate by holding a vision of myself at my favorite age.

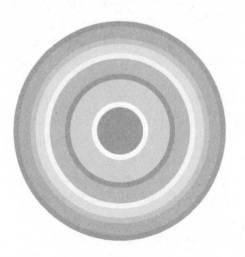

chapter thirteen

PEACE

THE GOOD SIDE

Every bad guy has a good guy inside.

AN OPEN LETTER TO THE LEADERS OF THE WORLD:

On one hand, we want to thank you. You have provided us with such adversity and it is this that has finally made us stronger. You have been formidable foes, but we are learning that this world will get better only when we love our fellow travelers and see the good in each one of them. We know that every bad guy has a good guy inside. And we know that spark of divine essence that dwells deep within our own Beings, also lies deep within yours.

If you were to come and join us at our table, you would find curiosity, friendship, and forgiveness. Just because you have treated us badly does not mean that we hold a grudge against you. We would, however, expect you to understand that we reject your authority and that you will find no support for your plans and schemes among us. We simply no longer choose to be manipulated.

Although there will be obstacles, we are willing to start over. We are prepared to be responsible for our own lives now. We must discard your cards, vaccines, and chip implants because they have too many strings attached. We must turn off your television and radio programs until their messages become uplifting. And we will start to rebuild our lives, without your help, by first living together in small, self-sufficient communities. If need be, we will grow our own food in our backyards as well as in common areas, and we will barter and trade among ourselves. We will also nurture our children with foresight, and learn to love and heal each other so peace and freedom can return to all of our lives.

As we see it, you are also being stalked by your own evolution and you will change. You cannot avoid being drawn out of your secrecy at this time. The only path left for you to follow is one of conscience. Like us, you are realizing that there is no separation between you and what you perceive. We are all beginning to understand that when we inflict pain or hardship on others, we inflict it upon ourselves. Once you fully comprehend what you are doing to yourself, you won't be able to continue. Enlightenment is coming to all who renounce conflict and violence. Even an unscrupulous, sophisticated robber baron can evolve into a higher, more loving entity. He is no less entitled to the Grace of our Great Creator than the people he has conspired against.

Just that one small transformation in your attitude whereby you begin to see, without blinders, that you only lack the opening of your heart in order to take the next step—a step for which you are poised and ready, but which all of your power and money cannot provide for you. Isn't that ironic, now, that you have dared for generations to hide our own hearts from us? Ever since we were trusting little schoolchildren reciting your pledges and practicing your patriotic ceremonies, you deceptively taught us to place our hands over our hearts on the left side of our chests! Only now are we locating our hearts in the exact center of our chests, and we are learning how to activate the wondrous feelings that have long slept dormant within us.

The people of the Earth yearn for the day when we will all live together in peace. You cannot stop us from advancing toward the love we all deserve. That glorious moment nears, when, instead of being adversaries, we will stand together as brothers and sisters whose consciences have awakened, as equals whose time of Heaven on Earth has come. Until then, for all the people who needlessly suffer and die because of your economic and political manipulations; for all the animals who face extinction or life in a cage that doesn't even allow them enough space to turn around; and for all the beautiful plants and trees of the forests who burn indiscriminately, we ask one last question: Why must you continue to bring harm and havoc to all the living things of the Earth when your own truest happiness would automatically come from helping us instead?

> **MY INTENTION FOR TODAY IS:**
> . . . .
> *I Intend that I am seeing everyone,*
> *including the current world managers,*
> *in their highest light.*

OUR TRUE HEROES
. . . .

Not one among us would deny mercy unto themselves.

Whatever happened to our sense of mercy? We've become too far removed from it. We've forgotten what it can do for us. Of all the human attributes to have lost contact with, it's a shame to have misplaced mercy. Where there is no mercy, soon learning will cease. Mercy is the one response that everyone seeks. Not one among us would deny it unto themselves. And yet we consistently deny it to our brothers, sisters, and neighbors. Why?

Nobody teaches about mercy anymore. The schools don't include it in their curriculums. Many churches advocate mercy, while they are quick to brandish the sword. The media has declared outright war on mercy. The hard line is followed; the ax must fall. Revenge is glamorized and the cries of mercy drowned out by the explosions of gunpowder. It sells movie tickets and boosts TV ratings.

The Intenders subscribe to the idea that whatever we are putting our attention on tends to materialize. And so, if we continue to keep watching and glorifying theatrical dramas filled with vengeance, then we will have vengeance in our lives. Mankind awaits heroes who will discard vengeance and resolutely dispense mercy.

When this starts to happen, we'll see a change in our lives. Our fears will begin to vanish, replaced by feelings of peace and safety. It will happen soon. We'll turn the TV on and a new kind of story will be running. A woman, held down, cries for release from her captors. She begs in the name of all that is sacred and, within her persecutor, something clicks. He hears her cries and stops and walks away.

Or a child turns his head back over his small shoulder and screams at his father to stop. "Please Daddy, please! Don't hit me again! I'll do anything! I'm sorry! Please don't hit me again!" And the father, for the first time, really listens to his young son's calls for mercy. And he suddenly understands that everything he wants his son to grow up to learn will be taught better if he puts his arm down and lets his child go free.

And what of all the war movies that we praise so highly? Soon we will see the raging, blood-thirsty soldier stop and empathize just for a moment, just long enough to hear the impassioned pleas of the conquered man as he lies on his back helplessly facing the bayonet. And the soldier will have a change of heart. He will see in the beaten man a part of himself. He will let his enemy go to live out the rest of his natural life in peace and productivity. And he himself will go and kill no more.

Then, as the sun sets across the movie screen and the music rises to its peak, we will have a new kind of hero. A hero who practices mercy. A hero who really cares about each and every one of his fellow men. A hero who will change the way we listen to and look at each other. He will be famous because he is merciful. And tickets to see his movies will be sold out way in advance.

> **MY INTENTION FOR TODAY IS:**
>
> *I Intend that I am acting with mercy
> every chance I get and that I am only supporting
> those who are acting with mercy.*

MERCY

Who among you would deny mercy unto yourself?

Lee Ching helped us create the Intenders. What you may not know is that he is the archetype of mercy, the male counterpart to Kuan Yin who is the archetype of compassion. We thought you'd like to hear this very special story about him.

This man was the commander-in-chief of vast armies in a time that has long been forgotten in our current reckoning of history. He was both respected and feared as one of the most powerful men in the realm. At the time our tale begins, two great civilizations known as Atlantis and Lemuria had been involved in a series of wars for centuries, and, despite all efforts to bring peace to the land, no one of integrity had stepped forward to speak out on behalf of the true good of the people. The world situation was at a stalemate; a cycle of decadence and darkness prevailed.

Envision, if you will, a setting late one autumn afternoon toward the end of a particularly bloody battle in a valley that was strewn with bodies of brave men and women. With no sign of either side looking to retreat, the carnage continued unabated. The commander of the Lemurian army had fought relentlessly all day alongside his fellow soldiers and his sword was covered with the blood and sinew of fallen enemies. Though weary and wounded, he battled on, willing to fight until the last man was left standing or he himself was killed.

At a certain moment, with the twilight fast approaching, he found himself in a furious struggle with a very strong, courageous opponent. After almost twenty minutes of toe-to-toe combat against this formidable warrior, the Lemurian commander swung his mighty sword at his rival and connected. The brave man fell on his back; his helmet and sword flew to the ground beside him. Just as the great commander readied to run his sword through the defenseless man's chest, he paused for an instant to look into the face of his enemy. The soldier was just a boy, no more than seventeen or eighteen years of age, whose body had matured rapidly considering its years. The young man's eyes were filled with a terror beyond imagination; he knew that he was about to die.

Suddenly, as often happens when one is pushed to the limits of strength and endurance, the great commander's perception shifted. With his sword held high in the air, he glanced out of the corner of his eye at the bloody battle that raged around him. Arms and legs flailed in a strange slow motion-like dance, nearby shouts and screams seemed to come from far off in the distance. His entire awareness changed as a new power rippled through his body. He felt expanded into something much greater than he was just moments before. In that same instant, his knowledge increased dramatically—the future and past revealed themselves in one momentous flash. He looked down at the boy laying at his feet and saw into the depths of his young opponent's soul. This boy didn't want to die. He longed to be safe and warm in the comforts of his own home with his loved ones and family. He dreamt of once again running through the fields with the beautiful fiancée he left behind when he went off to war.

The great commander then saw a part of himself in the young man's eyes; he saw a part of himself in everything around him. A feeling of deep compassion, such as he had never known before, overcame him. He knew he could not move to kill the helpless boy because, in doing so, he would only be killing himself. He dropped his sword to the ground and walked away from the battle to the top of a nearby hill.

What happened next was told and retold, passed on from generation to generation for thousands of years. There, as darkness shrouded the land, he fell to his knees, vowing never to harm or kill again...and in that moment, he was enlightened. Immediately, the soldiers in the valley below stopped their fighting and looked to the glow on the hill. Ten thousand people witnessed the light as it became brighter and brighter and broke free from its connection with the Earth. The great commander slowly ascended to perhaps three hundred feet above the hill and then gently floated to a point directly over the center of the battlefield. Some said that he hovered there for only a short time, while others reported that it seemed like hours. However long it was, all of those present were bathed and purified in the crystal blue-white radiance that gently showered down on them from above. None who were there that evening would ever go forth to fight again. Mercy and a new respect for one's fellow man were reborn within the human experience.

In time, the hovering white light began to fade and an outline of the commander's body took shape again. He settled slowly to the Earth and beckoned the soldiers to step back and give him room. Directly, he approached the boy who had fallen defenseless beneath his sword earlier and held out his arms. The two embraced like long-lost brothers, and when they finally pulled apart, the great commander bid the boy to go home to his family and fiancée and live his life in peace.

As the story goes, all of the soldiers on both sides left their weapons lying on the ground that night and sat around campfires together in silence. The next morning they began their return home to their families, carrying with them the story of what had happened the day before. Word quickly spread far and wide of a new Savior who walked the land. The great commander had become a Christed Being, a warrior for the light, and, from that point on, everywhere he went people were transformed, as if by magic, into fulfilled, joyful human beings. The series of wars that had lasted for centuries came to a sudden halt. Atlantis and Lemuria flourished once again as they had before the senseless wars had started.

It would be another thirteen thousand years before mankind forgot about the power of mercy and the example that was set that night by the great commander. These two magnificent cultures and all of their wondrous architectural and scientific achievements would one day be washed beneath the ocean waves into the sea and lost forever. But that is not the end of our tale.

The great commander and Savior's teachings, after being forgotten for lifetimes upon lifetimes, are now returning to the people of the Earth. His messages are heard in quiet moments in the minds of those who call forth the return of mercy. More and more people each day are choosing to lay down their swords and set aside their control issues in favor of peace. More and more are urging their national leaders to stop bullying one another and take a stance for the highest interests of all mankind. We are beginning to understand that acts of compassion and mercy inherently vanquish fear and return us to safety and comfort. We are moving toward a better world.

Furthermore, it is now being heralded, in obscure writings here and there, that the great ascended commander himself will return one day in the near future to walk again among the people and show them the magnificent rewards that come to the merciful. Indeed, among the scribes who announce his return, there is one man who has faint memories—visions— of a lifetime long past when he lay, defeated and helpless, on his back with a great warrior standing over him, sword raised and ready to strike. And sometimes, in rare moments of even deeper contemplation, he remembers a pact made between his soul and the soul of the great commander. Their agreement was to come to Earth in times of unrelenting darkness and play out the roles of courageous rivals so that this message about the power of mercy could be given unto you.

MY INTENTION FOR TODAY IS:

I Intend that I am withdrawing the sword, and I am allowing others to go free without any further persecution or judgment on my part.

NATIONALISM

. . . .

We are all different but equal.

A common thread that runs through all of the Intenders writings has to do with our illusions and how we can extricate ourselves from them. As we have said many times, there is nothing wrong with harboring an illusion; it's just that when we become aware of its true nature, we make a conscious decision whether to continue to play with it or set it aside.

Somewhere along the line, you decided to have some fun and incarnate into a body, and before you knew it, certain rules and resistances became apparent. Life on Earth, though abundant with rich feelings and experiences, had its risks. A wide variety of illusions and games presented themselves and you said to yourself, "This looks interesting! I think I'll play this game for a while. Why not? Everybody else is playing it. When the time comes for me to set aside this silly amusement and return to the way I felt as a child, it won't be any problem."

So you jumped in with both feet, started giving names to everything around you (including yourself), agreed that a great many artificial boundaries were real, created false identities and relationships, arbitrarily gave power to other people which allowed them to control you, began making judgments, and so forth. Life went on and as the years passed, you became more and more enmeshed in your illusions. When the time arrived for you to set aside all your games and dramas, it turned out that it wasn't so easy. You'd been heavily programmed and developed habits that didn't want to go away.

Such is the challenge that faces most people today. They're playing games; some taking life less seriously, while others are passionately putting everything they have on the line. In both instances, however, most people have long forgotten the moment when they chose to start playing. Most are lost in the dramas.

Perhaps the most insidious dramas we take part in have to do with our identification and allegiance to a particular nation. We identify with this country or that, and in doing so, we isolate ourselves, to one degree or another, from everyone else in the world. We agree upon arbitrary, make-believe boundaries and tell ourselves that we are the good guys, while anyone else who lives outside of our country's boundary lines is not as good as us, or isn't as deserving of all good things as we are. God forbid that someday, someone wanders across one of our boundary lines in need of help, but instead of sharing and opening our arms to our fellow traveler, we rally our other misguided countrymen together and run the needy invader out on a rail.

Of all our illusions, nationalism seems to bring out the

worst in us. Our allegiance to it somehow gives us an instant excuse to wreck harm or havoc on our fellow men and women. We stumble blindly forward, rarely looking deep enough to see that our allegiance to our nation has its inherent costs to us; costs which are perhaps higher than we know. In its wake, nationalism leaves us living in constant fear, not only for our homes and possessions, but also for our very lives and the lives of our precious families. It asks us to set aside all of our noble human traits and align ourselves with those who would kill at the drop of a hat. It makes everyone who believes in it a barbarian, indistinguishable from the pillaging hoards of centuries past. Indeed, none who kill in the name of country can call themselves sane.

Fortunately, the truth is always there to free us from our insanity. The truth brings all illusions to light where they can be seen and acted upon from a higher, more loving perspective. In the case of nationalism, we need look no further than the fact that the Earth is home to all of us. We all live here and have as much right to enjoy our lives as the next person. We may be different in our appearances, our languages, values, and beliefs, but we are all equal—equal in the eyes of God, equal at the core of our Beings.

As we begin to see through the illusion that we are better than someone else, it loosens its grip on us, and we take the first step toward living in a world of comfort and peace. We take the first step back to our sanity.

MY INTENTION FOR TODAY IS:

· ·

I Intend that I am seeing everyone, everywhere, as equal, regardless of our differences.

SETTING AN EXAMPLE

· ·

Speak freely and know safety.

The law that our thoughts create our experiences is not just a law unto each isolated individual. It is just as applicable to our beliefs as a whole. When individuals begin to create a new, peaceful world, so will the human race, as a whole, create a paradise on Earth. In other words, when we all see that we can have the world we desire just by thinking that we can, it will manifest for us.

And then, there's also the icing on the cake. It can happen fast. It can happen in our lifetimes. We need not think that we are just making things better for future generations. We are also making things better for ourselves. It can start with the smallest spark, and, as quick as a wink, it can spread around the entire globe.

It only takes for each of us to start to see everyone else in their highest light...even the international bankers and power brokers who have used deceit and fear and all things horrid in order to maintain control over us. We so often forget that each man, no matter how bad we think he is, does indeed, without exception, have a shining Spirit deep down inside. To remember this and to act accordingly is the challenge of mankind today. For some reason—perhaps the desire of some to dominate others—we have overlooked our ability to see the good side of every man. We don't notice him in his highest light. We don't see him standing up for the Highest Good. And if we don't see him standing up for the Highest Good, he won't. He'll continue to ride roughshod over us as he pleases. But it is when we begin to see every man, even our enemies whom we have called "the bad guys" in the past, as standing up for the Highest Good, they will sooner or later reflect our expectations of them and step into their highest calling.

There is something deep within our inner nature that is called up when we are confronted by a man of principle, a man who speaks directly yet gently into the face of his friends and enemies alike, and doesn't back down. Something special happens in the psyche of the "bad guy" when he is confronted by someone who sets a noble example. It may be subtle at first, but after awhile, it will change him, just as when you keep chipping away large rock, eventually it turns into pebbles...or a statue of great beauty.

His heart will soften and his mind will recognize the wisdom in becoming one with others. Walls of separation will dissolve as the "bad guy" begins to follow your example and seek for his own highest light inside himself. And when he looks, he will find a world that is better than the one where he spent all his energy trying to control everything and everyone around him. He'll experience a feeling of great joy that was not available to him as long as he persecuted others.

And we'll all be much happier because, from then on, instead of continuing to deal with the challenges of how do we get along with each other, we can all start to work together on the challenges of how do we make our world as good as it can possibly be.

> ### MY INTENTION FOR TODAY IS:
>
> *I Intend that I am seeing*
> *everyone in their highest light.*

GOOD NEWS

. . . .

That which you think about all day long
is what you manifest. It's the Law.

From one perspective it appears we don't spend much of our time really putting our attention on the good things that happen in our world. We're either too distracted by life's twists and turns, or we've become numbed by the media, not realizing that the media has no intention of helping us create peace or happiness for ourselves. Indeed, the media people are simply an extension of those who are propagating all of our unrest. They have a vested interest in the status quo and their prevailing attitude is "Who wants to hear good news anyway? Good news doesn't raise our ratings, or make for good copy, or get people excited, etc."

Well I, for one, would love to hear the good news. I'd love to turn the channel or open the newspaper to a place where only good news is presented, a place where creativity, invention, personal success stories, and the like are shared and celebrated.

Make no mistake, I am not talking about the "good news" which is a precursor for scarcity and tragedy, such as, "It looks like the price of gas is going to top off at xx dollars per gallon this summer," or "It looks like fewer people will be getting such and such disease now that the new inoculations are ready for distribution." No, I'm not interested in these same old ploys that have, embedded within them, the seeds for future problems. After many years of being barraged by these kinds of statements, I've come to see that they are really reinforcing our beliefs in sickness and scarcity. Why else would we be talking about these things if we weren't being prepared to experience them?

He took a long swallow of his drink. "This new memo is just another example of their same old double-talk. I feel like they're getting us ready to drop the ASL (Accumulated Sick Leave) by telling us it's in pretty good shape. It's the same hogwash with the talk of war on the six o'clock news. They told us last winter that relations were improving with that place whose name I still can't pronounce. They treated it like good news. They said that there was very little chance of conflict. If there's no chance of conflict, then why do they bother to mention it at all? They were just setting us up, because, sure as can be, there's war now. Every time I hear the good news, I get a little nervous, Lena. If the ASL is in such good shape, then why are they even talking about it? I feel like it's a setup, a sneaky little ambush."

The good news I'm talking about doesn't have a downside. It only speaks of peace, of safety, of limitless creativity, of examples of people living in joy and harmony with Mother Earth and all her amazing creatures. Contrary to popular belief, there is no shortage of happy stories; in fact, there are so many that we could fill our good newscasts and the pages of our good newspapers many times over with them if we would but choose to do so.

I am absolutely certain that if we were to take the benefits we receive from all of the violence, suffering, and scarcity that we currently prize and perpetuate in our media and weigh it against all the benefits we'd receive from circulating the true "good news" stories of the day, it wouldn't be long before everything would change. Our whole world would come alive again in anticipation of the best news we could ever imagine.

Indeed, the added benefit of watching or reading the good news coverage is that it is self-fulfilling. The more of it we put our attention on, the more of it we will create.

MY INTENTION FOR TODAY IS:

I Intend that I am tuning out any news that doesn't feel good and that I am tuning into the good news in my life.

POSITIVE LANGUAGE

. . . .

You manifest what you say you want
and you manifest what you say you don't want.

When we express ourselves in a negative fashion, we draw the exact opposite of what we desire into our lives. An example of this is evident when we say that we don't want an accident or a sickness to occur. What most of us don't understand is that by talking about anything—whether we want it or we don't—we invoke it; we attract it into our experience.

You see people do this all the time. They'll be talking about something they wouldn't want to happen, and, sure enough, it happens. What they weren't aware of is that, in their thinking processes, they pictured it happening. Since their thoughts are always creating their future, they, in fact, brought it to life when they said they didn't want it to happen.

The antidote to having calamities and accidents befall you is to speak only in the positive, to be even more vigilant of what you're saying, and to stop yourself before you give voice to the negative. Then, you can replace the "I don't wants" and all the talk of calamities by saying what you do want. If, for instance, you catch yourself saying, "I don't want war," which, as you have learned, will only conjure up more aggression and violence; instead, you can say, "I intend that I am living in peace." As you phrase your words like this, you invoke only the positive. There's no possibility for war because you haven't mentioned anything about it.

Some thoughts play tricks on us, having us believe that we are keeping our undesired experiences at bay by voicing our resistance to them. Now, however, as we're beginning to explore, more closely, how our thinking and speaking works, we can see that we are undermining or sabotaging ourselves by all our negative talk; that we are the cause of our calamities by the fact that we talk about them.

> ### MY INTENTION FOR TODAY IS:
> . . . .
> *I Intend that I am speaking only in the positive.*

YOUR INHERITANCE
. . . .

That which you seek is as close as your hands and feet.

What does it mean that the meek shall inherit the Earth? And just who are the meek? One thing is for certain; the European-

American western way of life is not set up to produce a lot of meek people. Westerners are strivers, and the meek do not strive. They do not seek out ways to gain profit from their fellow man. They are not busy counting their dollars. They are not fighting wars, nor are they interested in a thing for the sake of its appearance.

This is not to say that people raised with a western outlook on life could not change their longstanding attitudes. They could become meek in the twinkling of an eye, but what would it take? First, they would have to see that their old ways are not working for them anymore; that they have done in the past is not bringing them as much satisfaction or fulfillment or love or pleasure as it used to. Letting go of the things that they were previously attached to would suddenly become a viable option. Then they would have nothing that was worth worrying about or fighting over.

To be meek, a person has to have within himself or herself the ability to sit still and remain quiet. This is the key that opens the door to our inheritance. We must be able to sit completely still at any given moment with no wiggling, talking, or taking a break to go shopping or mend the fences. Just sitting still and letting the rest of the world do whatever it wants to do. We assure ourselves of our inheritance when we are able to step aside of all the dramas going on around us. When someone else comes along and is telling sad stories about how bad things are in the world, the meek person only has to be still and, in doing so, he is not agreeing and reinforcing his friend's woes. He doesn't even nod in agreement because he knows that that will only serve to perpetuate the dramas and suffering. He listens objectively, and when the time is right, he withdraws to his place within, the place where all inner joy and happiness comes from.

It is not that he has no compassion or feeling for his fellow man; but he must have the wherewithal to know where the road he is on is taking him. He no longer chooses to tread where he could easily become embroiled in the suffering that surrounds him. He no longer chooses to allow anyone else to dump any excess negative emotional baggage in his lap. He's done that before and it didn't work then because it left him feeling uncomfortable. He wants to be free from all of that, especially since freedom is so close within reach. He doesn't need to go anywhere or do anything. As a person learns to quietly and calmly meditate, all the joys that he could possibly imagine will emerge to lighten his load and uplift him into realms he never before dreamed of.

There will surely come a time in the lives of each of us when we must choose to pursue our old ways of struggle or strife, or we can decide to remain meek. Perhaps all we would have to do in order to receive our inheritance is sit down and be still.

> ## MY INTENTION FOR TODAY IS:
> . . . .
> *I Intend that I am learning to observe*
> *my surroundings without judging.*

TIMING
. . . .

Whatever needs to be known will be revealed
in the exact moment you need to know it.

How often do we stress ourselves out because we think we know how long something is going to take, and then it takes longer than we expected? We see this all the time and yet we do ourselves a tremendous disservice by setting time related goals. For, from the moment we go past the time parameter we have set for ourselves, we tend to take on unnecessary emotional charge. For some, this charge acts as a small nuisance, but for others they see themselves as "running behind" or "having to play catch up all the time." What they aren't realizing is that they never would have built up any emotional charge in the first place if they hadn't set any predetermined time limits for themselves.

The truth of the matter is that we never really know how

long something is going to take. We can guess, but in guessing we run the risk of needlessly upsetting our inner balance. If we would remember this, we'd save ourselves a whole lot of self-imposed stress.

The next time you make an intention—it doesn't matter what it is—resolve, at the same time, that you're willing to wait as long as it takes for it to manifest. Do this for a few of your intentions, then step back into a state of divine nonchalance, knowing that whatever you're intending is coming to you in its perfect timing. Now you're free to experience patience, and one of the first things you'll discover is that stress is not as much a part of your life as it once was. It's gone by the wayside because peace of mind has stepped in and taken its place.

MY INTENTION FOR TODAY IS:

*I Intend that I remember that everything
is happening in its perfect timing.*

THE GODSPARK

It'll all come together.
Just smile and watch it all come together.

You can call it the Godspark, the hundredth monkey, the reunion, critical mass, or whatever you like, but regardless of what you call it, it is coming. People are going to be lifted up and out of this encumbered mindset into a freer, more exalted place. We may or may not leave this Earth; however, the days of being a slave to another man's whims, the days of having our happiness tied to how much money we have, the days of us harming ourselves for reasons we are unaware of are coming to an end. It will be a huge relief, and a release such as we have never felt before. We'll wake up one morning, and everywhere you go you'll see people happy and smiling because they will be being given everything they need freely and lovingly.

Consider what happens when you strike a match. There is a critical point when just enough friction occurs to cause a spark to spring forth and a fire that wasn't there a moment before to burn brightly in front of you. It's the same with mankind as we move into the new millennium. It doesn't take all of us to bring about the change; it just takes enough of us to intend that we live in a world of peace and freedom and joy. It will happen in an instant. One moment we may still be shuffling through the shadows, and then, suddenly, in the next moment, one inspired person breaks a lifelong pattern and opens up to the Highest Good—and with this simple act of love, the entire human race reaches a critical point. A spark of light flickers, then bursts into flame, heralding a new standard and the life that we all deserve to live.

That person could be you.

MY INTENTION FOR TODAY IS:

I Intend that I am completely and utterly free.

THE MARRIAGE OF MIND AND MATTER

By your thoughts you shall be fulfilled.

One of the most common questions we get has to do with people having a difficult time marrying what's going on in their mind and what's going on outside of them. They tell us that they just can't seem to hold a vision of their Intention having already manifested, when the evidence in their outside world doesn't support that line of thinking. In answering these questions I'm reminded of one of my favorite characters in my latest novel, *The Reunion: A Parable for Peace*, namely Chief Seattle. To me, Chief Seattle embodies the attitude of staying positive regardless of his external situation better than anyone. Indeed, he knows how to hold his attention on the end result as if it is already done and manifested. I share his eloquent message with you here.

My brother, I tell you true. If all who see the Earth as being poisoned would, instead, give more attention to seeing the Earth clean and vibrant, then, very soon, your Earth would be cleansed.

If all who see their nation's leaders as misguided or uncaring would, instead, give more time to seeing themselves being represented by responsible, caring leaders who stand firm for the Highest Good of all, then, very soon, you would have good leadership.

If all who see their spouses or family members as troublesome or unloving would, instead, give more thought to seeing their loved ones as the shining children of God that they are, then, very soon, all challenged relationships would be renewed and love rekindled.

If all who see themselves as sick or poor or weak of heart or undeserving would, instead, give more energy to seeing themselves as healthy, abundant, empowered, worthy, and lifted up, then, very soon, they would experience all of the good things that life has to offer.

If all who see themselves as a physical body and no more would, instead, give more thought to seeing themselves as an ever-brightening star that resides inside the body, then, very soon, everyone in your world would be shining their lights—just as all of the elders who have walked your Earth have done. You would be living in peace, harmony, and comfort in a culture that you have created consciously, a culture, which by your divine right of birth, you deserve to enjoy.

Each challenge is there to guide you toward the desire
    of your heart.
Each problem, seen from the positive side, always turns
    into a blessing.
Each sorrow leads you to your joy.
Each doubt leads to your knowing.
Each lack leads to your abundance.
Each debt leads to your freedom.
Each feeling of hopelessness leads to your power.
Each cry of pain leads to your comfort.
Each act of war leads to your peace.
Each act of anger leads to your love.
And each journey through darkness leads into the light.

> ## MY INTENTION FOR TODAY IS:
> . . . .
> *I Intend that I am holding a vision in my mind*
> *of my Intentions having already manifested.*

PEACE

. . . .

Peace is just a thought away.

One of the subjects that seems to monopolize much of our thoughts today is defense or personal safety. In the spirit of helping us to understand how we are sabotaging ourselves in this area by holding onto our old ways of thinking, we will now address this highly charged topic by going a little deeper into our defense mindset.

When you're thinking that someone else is going to attack you, you are actually helping to create that attack. A defensive position always invites an attack. It works like this: In your mind, you're picturing someone—perhaps it's an enemy foot soldier, a renegade terrorist, or a drugged-out street criminal—coming to get you. This is a thought, just like all other thoughts. With enough attention put on it, it will work its way toward the surface of your experience, just like the thought that you're going to go to Disneyland next month.

Fortunately, we can pick any thought we want. Thoughts that serve us, and those that don't are equally available to us. If a person envisions attackers, then he will be attacked. If a person envisions Disneyland, then he'd better get his tickets ready. The question is: What kind of world do we want to live in? If we keep envisioning the same old us-versus-them separation scenarios as propagated by the media, then we'll never live in peace. But, if we shed our victim mentality and begin to picture our world in its highest light, then things will change. Thousands of years of man killing his fellow man will come to an end and be replaced by the expression of a deep and abiding respect for one another. All it takes is a little deeper thinking.

We must stop letting those with their own personal agendas tell us who our enemies are. We must investigate a little further to discover who the true perpetrators of violence on this planet are. And we must reject their manipulative suggestions and begin to discern in favor of that which is for the Highest Good of all.

For those who want to live in true freedom (not the kind of freedom offered by most present-day patriotic movements), peace needs to take the highest precedence. We must, in fact, demand peace because freedom requires a peaceful environment in which to grow and thrive. As of yet, not enough of us have been able to garner the inner strength needed to create a lasting peace. There are a few, and more are seeing the light every day, but it takes a larger number of people to stop supporting a social reality that doesn't serve them before a shift into true collective sovereignty will occur.

The time will come, in our very near future, when one more person envisions a peaceful world and, with that seemingly tiny action, the scales are tipped. The storm clouds disappear and a new world, the world that we deserve to live in as our right of birth, opens up before us.

It will be like a miracle but it's not really a miracle. It's only us having changed our thoughts.

MY INTENTION FOR TODAY IS:

*I Intend that I am guided, guarded,
and protected at all times.*

chapter fourteen

ONENESS

THE MAGICAL FLOW

*You need not be concerned about the future—
only the Now.*

THE FIRST TIME I CONSCIOUSLY EXPERIENCED THE magic of the present moment B. J. and I were building a rock wall together. We'd just hired our friend, Toshi, to bulldoze a new driveway on our property and when he was finished, the lower side of the road needed to have a retaining wall constructed to keep the Kona afternoon rains from washing away the dozer work. We had plenty of large rocks strewn about the land and, since they were free, we decided to use them to build the wall.

When we began, B. J. showed me how to dig a flat footing, which was about forty feet long, put up the batter boards and set the strings so the wall would be straight. At the time, it looked to me like it would take us weeks to complete the job.

With the preliminary work accomplished, he started placing the rocks with the flattest side of each one facing outward and leaning ever so slightly into the hillside. My job, since I was new at this, was to gather the best rocks and have them ready for him to set in line. Needless to say, at first, the job crept along very slowly. My work skills at that time were minimal, to say the least, primarily because I had never really done much manual labor before. As a result, B. J. spent a lot of time idle, waiting for me to bring him the rocks he needed.

After about an hour of painstaking labor, we took a break and sat with our backs against the first few stones he'd set into place. The view of the entire southern Kona coast spread before us like a picture of paradise. B. J. wasn't enjoying it like I was, however. He was staring at me with a disapproving smirk on his face.

"Didn't anyone ever show you how to work with someone else?" he asked me.

"No." I wasn't sure where he was going with this.

"Well," he said, "if we keep up our present pace, we'll be here all summer, building this wall. You've got to wake up!"

B. J. could be very blunt at times. I'd learned not to take everything he said personally, but sometimes it was hard. He knew how to push my buttons, and when he initially introduced me to The Information, I agreed to allow him to test me so I could see my weaknesses and eventually be free of all my buttons. Little did I realize, when I made that agreement, that B. J. was a Master at button pushing. More than a few times, I'd end up walking away from a heavy conversation with him, muttering and cussing about how he could be such a jerk to insult and belittle me like he did.

I was just about ready to walk away this time, too, when he caught me, only now he spoke in a gentler, softer tone of voice. "One of the biggest problems in America today," he said, "is that people don't really know how to work together. We've got all sorts of fancy, highfalutin educational systems and we soak up tons of knowledge, but very few are able to put it to good use."

I listened because I needed the rock wall built. But my ego, which was puffed up because I had a college degree, wanted to scream in reaction.

"People are too isolated from one another nowadays," he went on. "They work by themselves, often in little cubicles, and never discover the joy that can come from working as part of a team. They never get to step into the magical flow which comes when two or more are concentrated on a common project."

Now, I thought to myself, we're getting somewhere. The magical flow sounded interesting to me.

"There's a coming together—a Oneness—that can occur whenever two people are working together and putting their attention on the same thing," he said. "It doesn't matter if they're in an office, on an assembly line, or working in a tool and dye shop. In our case, it can happen right out here in the middle of the rainforest, while we're building this rock wall. But, we'd have to take extra care and keep an eye on what the other one is doing at all times."

"I can do that," I said, glibly.

"Well, up until now, you haven't," he responded. "If we're going to work together, and have any hope of stepping into the magical flow, you'll have to pay much closer attention to what I'm doing and make sure you have the next rock ready for me when I need it. Otherwise, I'll be sitting around, twiddling my thumbs, while you're off in the woods somewhere, doing God knows what!"

The bluntness had returned, but blunt or not, I knew he was right. And besides that, my interest was piqued. I wanted to check out the magical flow. So, from that point on, not only did I gather rocks, I also watched what he was doing. It involved me having to do two things at once, but, with a little practice, I found that I was able to have the perfect rock sitting right there for him, so he didn't have to move more than six inches to pick it up and place it in the wall.

By the time we took our next break, the sun was high overhead and, without me even noticing, several hours had passed. I'd been so focused on the project at hand that it was like the rest of the world had gone away. I never worked so hard and felt so good! I'd experienced a state of Oneness, as sweet as any I'd ever had in my meditations or prayers. And, to top it all off, when I looked around me, there were fifteen feet of wall, five feet high, already backfilled and standing at the end of the day. A whole lot of work had gotten done while we were in the magical flow.

MY INTENTION FOR TODAY IS:

I Intend that I am in the flow where Great Mystery and Miracles abide.

WE ARE ALL ONE

We are our own ancestors.

Looking at things from a higher level, we live in a body for a while, then discard it, only to take on or inhabit another body again when the time is right. We do this over and over for the purpose of experiencing all that we can. We get ourselves into tight places, and then find our way out. We are the good guys until that gets boring enough, then we are the bad guys until we learn our lessons there. And on and on it goes.

When we are able to see the larger picture, we discover that we are incarnating into body after body, lifetime after lifetime, and from this perspective, we leave a legacy to ourselves. When we do something to make this world a better place for our children or for future generations, we are really making it a better place for ourselves. Indeed, we are the ones who come back, time and time again, to harvest the fruits of our own labors.

That's one point of view. Here's another: at its purest essence, the Being, or Entity, or Spirit (or whatever you'd like to call It) that resides inside your body is the same Spirit that resides in everybody else's body. Outwardly, we have different identities, different preferences, different physical characteristics, different formative programming, different cultural influences, different astrological configurations, different genetics, different strengths and weaknesses, different you name it, but one thing we all have in common is the core template we start out with. At the center of our Beings, we are the same, and in some mysterious way, a connection, which is typically kept hidden from us, exists between the Being inside our body and the Beings inside every other body we see. Just as one drop of water is part of the whole ocean, so is one person's Spirit part of a much larger, vaster, collective Spirit that is made up of all Spirits. When our differences are put aside, and our connections to each other are brought to light, we see ourselves in everyone else. We know that we are one, and that the good works we leave as a legacy for others is really a legacy we are leaving to ourselves.

Know this and be comforted: We purposely do not tell you who we are or where we come from. Our experience has taught us that if we do, some of you will tune us out, even though we are on the same team. We will tell you that we stand strong for the Highest Good, just like you, and that we have met, face to face, with you on many occasions that you do not presently remember. You are one of us and we take good care of our own. We agreed, long ago, to come here to Earth in this place and time to make life better for all and everyone. Soon you will see, as you begin to integrate The Code into your life, that it feels familiar to you. That's because it's a reminder you left to yourself.

MY INTENTION FOR TODAY IS:

I Intend that I am remembering who I really am.

COMMUNITY
. . . .

In order for humanity to reach its highest calling,
people must come together.

The Universe places people in front of us who we are supposed to help. The question then becomes, how can we best do this? We're not really serving others when we allow them to become dependent on us for an indefinite period of time. Nor do we further ourselves. If we allow ourselves to become a crutch for others, we deny them the life experiences that will lead them to their own empowerment, and we deny ourselves the energy and freedom we need to do our life's work to its fullest potential.

Many people come to our community who are needy. From their point of view, life has thrown them a curve, but from where we stand, we see this as an opportunity for both of us to move forward. We know that some will fit in our circle and some will not. Those who don't fit in here will eventually find another path that suits them better. Like many Native American tribes, we always provide them with food and the tools for becoming self-reliant. We will do our best to teach them the Intention Process and how to use their thoughts and words in a way that will serve them. They will be welcomed into our Intention Circles where they can rub elbows with others like themselves who are steadily learning to manifest the things that they desire. And, if they are ready and open to receive, they, too, will begin to manifest things and become self-empowered.

Empowerment is something that we carry with us. We need not be tied to a certain place or a particular group of people in order to become a Mighty Manifester. Once a person lets go of the blame game and starts to feel the gratitude that accompanies the manifestation of their intentions, he or she can go anywhere and use the Intention Process. They can start an Intenders Circle at the next stop on their journey and pass on what they have learned to others who are ready for it.

A community is not defined by its physical boundaries. In fact, the strength of a community lies in its ability to spread out. Kept confined, a community will soon begin to decay. The enthusiasm for life will soon become stifled without adequate room to expand. Of course, we could have an exclusive community where we set a limit as to how many people we will allow in. But this attitude promotes the very separatism that is the cause of the quandary that humanity faces today.

These are not the times for exclusivity or for people to remain isolated from each other. We all need each other. Our Intenders Community is one where people can come, get empowered, and go on their way. We give them an Intenders Handbook for occasional reminders, the experience of the power of the Intenders Circle, and we trust that the Universe will take good care of them as they take their next step in life.

> ## MY INTENTION FOR TODAY IS:
> . . . .
> *I Intend that I am discovering the benefits*
> *that community has to offer.*

NETWORKING

. . . .

You can tell a live wire by its connections.

Many of you are catalysts. In the times to come you will have a lot to do with communities and getting people together so that they can help each other. There are many groups scattered around the Earth who do not know that others like themselves even exist. In your travels, you're going to help to bring them together so they'll know about each other and know about each other's good works.

You will find these grassroots groups to be as small as a handful of dedicated people or as large as a community of thousands. They will go by many different names; some may call themselves Intenders of the Highest Good, while others call themselves the Garden Club. It doesn't matter what they're named as long as they're open and following some sort of positive, uplifting belief system.

People always benefit from finding out what other people have done. It isn't necessary to remake the wheel every time we turn around. There are people in Greenpeace and the Audubon Society and the Sierra Club and many, many more who are working hard to preserve our precious environment. There are amazing connections from Virginia Beach to the Four Corners to Mount Shasta who are exploring the highest potentials of the human being. They all have something wonderful to share with you. You can visit these groups and take the lessons that you have learned back to your own community.

And there is the Internet. It is full of people who are ready to help you. It abounds with talk of new ideas that wouldn't otherwise come to the surface in the mainstream media. You can go into a search engine and, in a matter of seconds, find out about everything from free energy sources to meditation techniques. As long as it remains unregulated by those who would seek to control others, it will bring more and more freedom into our lives.

If you are part of a community and you find yourself traveling around the countryside or browsing the World Wide Web, know that wherever you are, there is a message there for you. Sometimes you may have to pay very close attention, but be assured that you can learn something valuable from whatever you are doing. Then you can keep the flow going by sharing it with others.

Every community needs its catalysts, its live wires. It's easy to tell these live wires by their connections. When it's time for your group to spread its wings, you will have connected with people who've already been through what you're going through. They will help you and you will help them. You will become a part of them, and they'll become a part of you. And, pretty soon, we will have all come together in the name of abundance and peace and harmony for all mankind.

MY INTENTION FOR TODAY IS:

I Intend that I am bringing people together whenever I can.

PROJECTIONS

It appears to be dualistic, but it is not.

Where do our thoughts and feelings come from? We tend to think that they all originate from us, and from the point of view that it's all one (or it's all God), that is true. Realistically, however, most of us are caught up in our Earthly lives, having forgotten what it's like to experience the Oneness of all things. We have separated ourselves from our surroundings, and then extended that separation by naming and defining all of the objects and creatures around us.

Of course, there is absolutely nothing wrong with that. It's all here for us to enjoy; however, we tend to get mixed up when we ascribe the properties of one world onto another. Said another way, we get confused when we tell ourselves that it's all God, and then, in the very next moment, someone crosses our path and we find ourselves making a judgment of them. It might help if we were to explore where the judgment originated.

Our judgments (and their accompanying feelings) come from one of three places: 1) from us; 2) directly from others; 3) from the great etheric substance that invisibly surrounds us. If a judgment is originating from us and we are holding onto it, we can be assured that we have some strong prejudices that need to be addressed before we are going to evolve into a lighter state of being. Indeed, judgments can only happen in a world where separation exists. There has to be a "me" and a "them" if a judgment is occurring, and such an arrangement keeps our Oneness at bay.

Many of our judgments do not originate with us. As an example, I went into the post office yesterday to mail my book orders, and as I approached the lady behind the counter I had the thought, "Her hair sure looks weird." Now, a part of me is trained to refrain from making judgments and to see everyone in their highest light, so I immediately wondered where that thought came from. The first answer I came up with was that it was coming directly from her. She was projecting it, and I was just picking up on her projection. That kind of thing happens all the time, especially when we are in direct contact with others.

Or, it could have come from the "air" around me, the ethers we are all "swimming" through all the time. Our streets and roads are littered with thought projections. We get impatient or mad in traffic, often thinking that our angry feelings and thoughts are coming from us, when, in truth, they are coming from the collective etheric stream of fearful thoughts that inhabit the areas we're driving through. Projections of others engendering road rage, or fender benders, or being followed or pulled over gather around our highways and byways, and we move through this invisible stream every time we drive somewhere. In other words, it's not us; we're just using our mental and emotional antennae to pick up on the projections that have been placed there in the past.

Here's what Lee Ching had to say about this awhile back:

"When you become a truly conscious Being, you will have moments of relapse when you'll forget where your good is coming from and old rules will come to the surface. It is like when you are looking into the eye of the dragon; there is much goodness and nobleness in the dragon and, at the same time, it can be the dangerous fire-breather as well. These are simply the dualities that face this world today, that face people like yourselves who have the highest and best good involved in their lives—in wanting to talk to people, and wanting to feel free to move about this world, and wanting to help people understand what it is they're creating with their everyday thoughts.

These things are noble causes and, like with the dragon, it is the noble and good side that calls forth the peaceful warrior. There are times when people must take up the position of the warrior to create peace because sometimes the dark can overcome the light. When you are a conscious Being, you know that it is all the same thing; you know that there is really no evil and there is no good; but you also know that there is always a battle going on between the conscious Beings and the unconscious Beings...the angel people and the animal beings."

MY INTENTION FOR TODAY IS:

. . . .

I Intend that I remember where my goodness
and my nobility are coming from.

THE POWER OF THE CIRCLE

. . . .

A circle of people is like a jewel box.
Place your Intentions in it.

I was making some phone calls yesterday to set up workshops for our upcoming tour, and noticed that we'd had several orders recently from Tulsa, Oklahoma. Encouraged by this, I called the Intenderpreneur there, a happy, jovial man named Clifford, and I asked him how his Intenders Circle was doing. His reply was short and to the point.

"Oh, we don't meet regularly anymore," he said.

Well, this was not what I expected to hear, especially since he had just been added to our directory of Intenders Circles only three months earlier. I didn't know what to say. It was not a response I was accustomed to hearing. Then, he went on.

"It worked," he said. "We got everything we intended for right away." And then he proceeded to tell me several inspiring stories about how he and his friends had manifested new homes, jobs, and more for themselves. As it turned out, everyone in his Intenders Circle had been friends before they were introduced to the Circle, and the only thing missing whenever they'd previously gotten together was a workable, user-friendly format. Now that they had become proficient at using the Intenders format, it was like the last piece in a puzzle snapped into place and the whole picture came into focus.

From that point on they decided to gather less often, but when they did come together, boy, were they powerful!

We started out with four of us sitting around a table on the patio once a week. We'd go around the circle and each of us would say our gratitudes and then our intentions for the things that we desired to manifest in our lives. Pretty soon, we were getting phenomenal results, a bunch of our friends had joined us, and the feeling of being part of a family had awakened in all of us. As the group got larger and larger, we began listening to each other even more closely. We became cheerleaders for each other, really being happy for someone else when their intentions came to life.

We also discovered a lot of joy in keeping a watchful eye out for the things that others in our circle had intended to manifest. Bartering, trading, and sharing became commonplace, and we felt a new strength now that we were part of a network where everyone was helping everyone else. The Intention Process was working and our lives changed quickly for the better!

> **MY INTENTION FOR TODAY IS:**
>
> . . . .
>
> *I Intend that I am enhancing*
> *my manifesting skills by gathering regularly*
> *with lighthearted and like-minded friends*
> *in an Intention Circle.*

THE INTENDERS CIRCLE

. . . .

In order to have peace, freedom,
and a high-quality living environment for ourselves,
people must come together.

Deep inside each of us, we know that a better world awaits us when we stop separating ourselves from one another. The competition in the marketplace, political standards, self-serving media scenarios, and so forth have continually worked to keep us apart from our fellow man, but have not brought us happiness in return. The path to our ultimate empowerment calls for us to come together. We must begin to take advantage of the strength that comes from sharing our intentions.

That's what the Intenders Circle format does. You don't need to follow it to the letter. In fact, we suggest that you check it out and adapt it to what works best for you. Many groups, for instance, simply don't have the time for a potluck, and to them we say, "Don't let that stop you. Come together and combine your intentions anyway. You'll be very glad you did."

When the Intenders first started getting together, we experimented with many different formats and agendas. It was easy to tell which ones worked because we'd hear the expressions of gratitude right away. When something didn't work, we didn't hesitate to discard it immediately.

The eight-step format listed below is the one that most Intenders Circles use today. It is this unique format that has made the Intenders so successful. Thousands of people from all over the world have experienced profound results by following our friendly format. Whether you're a small circle of friends coming together for the first time, or you're an already established group of people who have been meeting regularly for years, we suggest that you test this format for yourselves.

THE INTENDERS CIRCLE FORMAT

1. First, we bless our food.

2. Second, we have a potluck because we've found that sharing food together is a wonderful way of bringing people, especially strangers, together.

3. Third, we have a short, guided meditation in order to balance and center ourselves.

4. Fourth, we briefly explain the Intention Process to our newcomers. Some Circles do this before the circle begins by showing the Intenders video to those who come early.

5. Fifth, we go around the Intention Circle and everyone shares their gratitudes and intentions.

6. Sixth, we make an invitation, calling forth invisible helpers who stand for the Highest Good and we tone.

7. Seventh, we take a fifteen- to thirty-minute break for more eating and socializing.

8. And eighth, we have our spiritual guidance session where we read, listen to tapes or to an inspiring messenger. Not every group does this, but those who do seem to evolve faster.

MY INTENTION FOR TODAY IS:

*I Intend that I am coming together
with my fellow travelers
for the Highest Good of All concerned.*

SOME COMMON QUESTIONS
ABOUT THE INTENDERS

*Sometimes you need the help of a friend
until you can move mountains again.*

We also get asked regularly about what to call your Intenders Circle. Some people prefer calling themselves the Milwaukee Intenders, for instance, while others may already have a good name, like the Unity Study Circle or the St. George Ascension Group. Still others may not want to have a name at all. When we're asked about this, we always say that it's not what you call yourselves that's important, rather it's the getting together that matters. You can call yourselves anything you like.

How often to meet is also a common question. It seems that some Circles just can't get together once a week, and that is okay. In our Intenders Circle in Pagosa Springs, we met once a month last winter because the snow was so deep. The main thing is that you do gather at least monthly, if for no other reason than to hold the light for your area.

Most people don't realize that the feeling of Oneness you get at the end of an Intenders Circle is a very unique experience. Some would say it is sacred and is to be treated with great respect. Certainly, when you return to a place where you've called in a pillar of light and toned together on past occasions you can feel a crispness in the air. Just as memories are stored in the objects around you, so are the feelings you've created in an Intenders Circle kept intact so that the next time you come together it is easier for you to reach the states of joy and empowerment you seek.

The elders of the Native American tribes know that their thoughts and feelings are infused into the places they visit. In fact, that's one of the reasons why they go to the tops of the mountains. Not only are these places isolated and peaked, but they are also humming with power and energies left there by ancestors who reached higher states of awareness by praying there in the past. Knowing that, the elders send their brave young men and women to the mountaintop for their vision quests because the thoughts and feelings in the boulders make it easier for the young initiates to experience a good connection with Great Spirit.

MY INTENTION FOR TODAY IS:

I Intend that I am creating sacred spaces for myself and others everywhere I go.

YOUR NEXT STEP

The Highest Good always leads you to Love.

In the Intenders, you have been practicing, making ready for a great change in the way you live. You will know this change because it will be brought on by a wondrous event, an event that will be characterized, in part, by a Reunion—a reuniting of long-lost friends, both seen and currently unseen, for the purpose of fulfilling agreements and arrangements you made eons ago.

Those of you who have been working to bring this event into manifestation by your meditating, sincere prayers, and conscious intentions will recognize each other, first and foremost, because you will all be standing firm for the Highest Good together. In letting the Highest Good be your guide, you will not be accompanied on your path for long by those who would continue threatening, controlling, or seeking to make you afraid. Those you will meet at the Reunion will be greeting you with open arms, as family, wanting only to help you and lift you up in the Spirit of Love. The Highest Good always leads you to Love.

MY INTENTION FOR TODAY IS:

*I Intend that I am open
to reunite with my soul's family.*

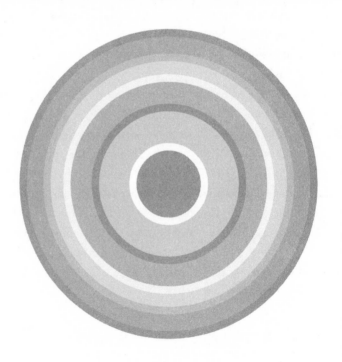

chapter fifteen

FINALE

A POP QUIZ

You are here to gather light and spread it to the world.

Here is a fun pop quiz for you. Let's see how you do. The answers are upside down in the graphic at the bottom. Get twenty of them right, and you're a Mighty Manifester!

1. Choose the one that will work best:
    A.) I intend that I get a new car.
    B.) I want a new car.
    C.) I intend that I have a new car now.
    D.) All of the above.

2. Which will give you the best outcome?
    A.) Don't forget to take out the trash.
    B.) Remember to take out the trash.
    C.) I'll get the trash later.
    D.) All of the above.

3. Which response will give you the best results?

    A.) I intend that there is no more war.

    B.) I intend to live in peace.

    C.) I intend that I am living in peace now.

    D.) All of the above.

4. Which will give you the best outcome?

    A.) I feel like I'm getting sick.

    B.) I intend that my cold doesn't last too long.

    C.) I intend that I am in excellent health.

    D.) The doctor says I have a cold but it will go away soon.

5. The best arrangement for empowering in a group of people is:

    A.) a circle.

    B.) an audience.

    C.) at desks and tables.

    D.) standing anywhere.

6. Which response will give you the best results?

    A.) I intend that I have conquered my fears.

    B.) I intend that I am not afraid anymore.

    C.) I'm becoming more brave every day.

    D.) I intend that I am courageous now.

7. Which will give you the best outcome?
     A.) I'm trying.
     B.) I'm hoping.
     C.) I'm wishing.
     D.) I'm intending.

8. What is the best dedication to end your intentions?
     A.) For the Highest Good.
     B.) For the Higher Good.
     C.) For the Greater Good.
     D.) Any of the above.

9. Which of the following are not illusions?
     A.) I am thirty-eight years old.
     B.) I am a nurse (or a teacher, or an architect).
     C.) I am from Denver.
     D.) I am.

10. Choose the one that will work best:
     A.) I intend to be happy.
     B.) I intend that I am not unhappy anymore.
     C.) I intend that I am happy.
     D.) I wish I was happy.

11. Things may not have manifested for you because:

    A.) the timing isn't right yet.

    B.) you're still harboring some doubts.

    C.) it's not in your Highest Good.

    D.) all of the above.

12. Your desires:

    A.) get in the way of things.

    B.) are in you for you to fulfill.

    C.) should be repressed and denied.

    D.) are not good for you.

13. You're most apt to build a stronger immune system by:

    A.) taking more vitamins.

    B.) eliminating negative emotions.

    C.) cutting alcohol out of your diet.

    D.) keeping up on your inoculations.

14. You can learn things by:

    A.) meditating.

    B.) imitating someone who already knows.

    C.) experience.

    D.) all of the above.

15. Diseases get worse by:
     A.) believing the doctor's diagnosis.
     B.) agreeing that they exist.
     C.) telling people that you have one.
     D.) all of the above.

16. If you are feeling down, you can feel better by:
     A.) singing.
     B.) praying or meditating.
     C.) toning.
     D.) all of the above.

17. The most fulfilling line of work is one where:
     A.) you enjoy it.
     B.) it helps others.
     C.) you enjoy it and it helps others.
     D.) you make a lot of money.

18. Which is most important?
     A.) Your money.
     B.) Your joy.
     C.) Your relationships.
     D.) Your possessions.

19. You are:
     A.) your body.
     B.) your name, address, and social security number.
     C.) the essence that is inside your body.
     D.) your historical data.

20. When you oppose others:
     A.) you become just like them.
     B.) you set an example for your friends.
     C.) you are showing them what is right.
     D.) you are making things better for everyone.

21. Which one will help your Aunt Sally the most?
     A.) Aunt Sally doesn't look too well.
     B.) The doctor told Aunt Sally she has fumbuckaruckus.
     C.) Aunt Sally has been having a lot of problems lately.
     D.) I'm seeing Aunt Sally in her highest light.

22. People working together can:
     A.) move the path of storms.
     B.) heal hospitals full of people.
     C.) live in freedom and peace.
     D.) all of the above.

MY INTENTION FOR TODAY IS:

· ·

*I Intend that I am answering
at least twenty questions correctly,
and that I am a Mighty Manifester.*

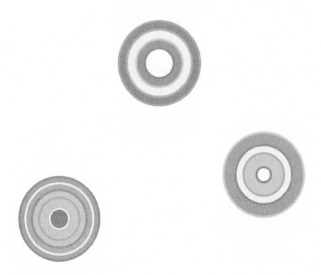

ANSWERS TO POP QUIZ:

1c. 2b. 3c. 5a. 6d. 7d. 8a. 9d. 10c. 11d. 12b. 13b. 14d. 15d. 16d. 17c. 18b. 19c. 20a. 21d.

347

"THE BRIDGE" MESSAGES THAT INSPIRED *GET WHAT YOU WANT* (WWW.INTENDERS.ORG)

Dear Tony,

This morning I read the Reminder #118 Humility and it touched my heart so much. I am writing to let you know that each and every one of your messages has been instrumental in my life and I appreciate them beyond words. Often when I am having difficulty, a message will come from the Reminders the very day that I had been praying for an answer. I have sent these around the world to friends who were searching for answers. You are a very special gift in our lives and I will always remain grateful to you. Have a grand and glorious day.

Kass Callaghan
Sonoma, CA

Tony,

Remarkable how these keep aligning with me in the exact moment. Can't thank you enough for these. Of all the subscriptions, blogs, message boards, ya-da, yours has been the most timely and powerful. Thanks for being you, and for the difference you make in this world.

Namaste
Ted Tilton
Colorado Springs, CO

Hello Tony,

I received this morning the Message #53 and I just want to thank you for these beautiful messages! This Reminder just reconfirmed what is happening right now in my life. The unlimited abundance that is available to us all; that we can speak directly to Him and all the love, joy and peace that we can experience if we but only open ourselves up to it. What an amazing experience it is for me! Thank you to you and the team assisting you with this great task of helping others in setting them free. May the Intenders go from strength to strength in the days to come.

Love, Joy, and Peace.
Arno Theron
South Africa

Hello Intenders,

Thank you so much for the wonderful messages that you send. I look forward to receiving them and they never fail to make me feel uplifted or prod me to change my thoughts about something so I can see it in a different way. I want you to know that you bless my life with these emails. Thank you!

Pat Yurick
Titusville, FL

Hello,

I wanted to show you what I did for my bible study group that meets at my house and who are all followers of Christ. Your writings clarify and help bring to life the reasons why Christ would say these things, and bring clarity to what would happen in the world if we would follow them. If organized religion focused on these things more, we would not be bombing people, we would be offering love instead. You are obviously being led by the Holy Spirit. Keep up the good work.

Wayne Canpsall

Hi Tony,

I have been blessed by your emails. I would love to help promote this important message. I already link to your site. I am starting an Internet radio show and would love to interview you. Would you be interested?

Blessings,
Lonna Bartley

I love you Tony Burroughs, you are such a pure, positive gift and I am so grateful to be connected with you. Thank you so much for all that you offer and give. Of all the teachers like those featured in *The Secret* and Abraham Hicks, what makes you so different and so refreshing is your utter sincerity, simplicity, and dedication to staying humble and real. I haven't yet found an Intenders Group in my area, but just reading your books and receiving your emails and putting the intention process to work in my life morning and night has produced amazing miracles and magic in my life and my kitties and my loved ones too! Take care and all the blessings from the Universe to you Tony, you rock!

Love,
Shelley Katrina

Amen, Tony!!

Reminder #81 is awesome! Thank you so much for all you are and all you do!

Blessings, Peace, Love,
Donna Jo Bergman
Mansfield, TX

Hello Intenders,

I have cried this morning with the pure gratitude of reading the story of the dog in Reminder #3. You go Rusty, I know where you are now—free.

Much love and light to you dear people at the Intenders,
Ellann Lehdey
Australia

Tony,

Thanks for *these messages*. *They* always resonate with me, today more than usual...synchronicity makes me aware that the magic of life is still alive.

Peace and Love,
Katy O'Leary
California

Hello Intenders,

Thank you, thank you, thank you! It always seems when I read *one of your messages* it's perfect for that moment...but today's was spot on! I have been lying awake at night wondering why this person is so mad and hurtful toward me. I've been really working on not taking it personal or reacting. Wow, thanks, I needed that! You're awesome and a true gift to the world!

Thank you from the bottom of my heart!
Kim Mazzuca
Federal Way, WA

Hi Tony,

You guys rock big time! I so love your messages! and am forever grateful and full of grace for your heart, your love, and your great, great inspirations of light and truth. Everything you share...everything...truly rings true in the depths of my soul. I feel so at home here, as I know so many of us do. It is such a sweet reunion and a very enlightened awakening to continue connecting with all these Intenders and bringers of the Light and of the most highest good for all.

Much, much gratitude, love and light,
Janice Patterson

My Brother,

I've been blind for 51 years, but thanks to normal sight for 12 years, was able to see what you so aptly created for me/us. Thanks for giving me those moments of sight. Like Rusty, I am now celebrating!

Lovenergy,
Joe Tolve
Connecticut

Tony,

I don't know if you've gotten to the point where you hear it too much, but I've really enjoyed your messages. Thank you.

Susan Kennedy

Hello Tony,

I have been getting these messages from the very first one, and I applaud all of you at Intenders Bridge for sharing such wonderful information. Eventually, and I know now when the timing will be right, I hope to set up an Intenders Circle here in the Bahamas.

Love, Light, Oneness,
Catherine Whitney

Dear Tony,

I think your messages are so profound and I look forward to them every day. I am touched by the depth and truthfulness that they contain. So sorry I haven't expressed my gratitude sooner. You are truly wonderful and appreciated! Please continue to spread your light!

Sherry Smith
Andover, MA

Hello,

This is just a quick message to say a great big thank you for all the messages to date, especially the reminder ones, and most especially the one I opened yesterday, No. 26, and this one today.

Love Light Joy Peace and Blessings,
Maryanne Gosling
Ireland

Hello Intenders,
Thank you...perfect timing.

Blessings,
Tammy Wilson

Hello and Thank you so much for sending me the New Reminders. I have the books, but the Reminders are a wonderful gift. They focus my thoughts on the truth and turn my day around.

In gratitude,
Lindsey Suleman

Hi!

My name is Rose Romero. I just wanted to express my gratitude for the Intenders of the Highest Good. Your Reminders are a big highlight for me and I intend to use the information and love daily in all things that I think and do. I have manifested things that I really wanted at the time. I believe that life is only getting better.

Namaste
Rose Romero Wechapi Luta Wi
Colorado Springs, CO

Greetings Tony!

Keep doing what you do—it is awesome, and it has changed my life this year!

Sincerely,
Layli Phillips

Hi!

I subscribe to the Intenders and have signed up my friends and family too. It's really making huge, wonderful differences in my life. Thank you! I bought The Code movie for my mom's 60th birthday early in October and love it. I also recite The Code daily. It makes me very happy and I always really "feel" it and smile while saying it out loud. Thank you again!

Katie E. Heath
Indianapolis, IN

Dear Tony,

I love getting your Intenders Bridge. They inspire me and remind me of my inner journey.

Love and Light and Blessings to you,
Samantha Brick
Australia

Hi,

I just wanted to let you know how much I appreciate the letters I receive from you, and I really did enjoy the one on Gratitude.

Thank you for doing what you do, it's priceless.
Gina Knop

My dear Intenders,

I too feel the way you have described in this Reminder #27. The journey continues to shed "old ways" and allows my self to be open to being guided through these tumultuous times. I thank you daily for your messages. It's good to have company and your company is good.

Ingrid Ruhrmann
Canada

Hello Intenders,

This is such a perfect message for all the light workers of the world to keep in mind. Especially timely for me today. Thank you, thank you, thank you for all your messages, for your insights, for your time, efforts, patience, and outreach. You are doing a great job! Your messages are so wonderful and uplifting that I have printed many out and put them on the fridge as reminders.

Thank you again,
Judy Galganski
Buffalo, NY

Dear Intenders,

Thank you, thank you, thank you for this #3 Reminder. I felt the sadness in every word of Rusty's story. I see it in my father's life story and, in many ways, in my own, until recently. I shall treasure #3 as a reminder of how close freedom always is.

Love and Light,
Lesley Gillett
Queensland, Australia

Hi Tony,

Keep up the good work! Thank God for those of you who have courage enough to speak out and give us something to think about.

Light from my Heart,
Donna Nixon

Tony,

I am deeply grateful for your letters, they encourage me, they uplift me, and every day it is like my soul is saying this is what you need to hear. Please keep writing! You are the light that shines and helps brighten my day. Thank you.

In gratitude,
Brenda P. Wilson

Hello Intenders,

Beautiful spirits of the "Intenders," your "Messages" have given me much strength and positive energy in my time of challenge and expansion.

Thank you, and blessings on your "journey of light."
Maria Irish

Hi,

The Intenders Messages are the best one can find anywhere. Thanks for spreading such highest level thoughts/wisdom to the people around the world.

Regards,
Girish Telang

Dear Intenders,

Just a little note to thank you all for the wisdom of your words. You send them freely to me, and I know it is from the heart. Continue your work, and may you all be blessed in this endearing project. We should all contribute to the awakening of our mother earth's children.

Light and Love to you!
Vivi Held

Good morning Tony,

I have just read Intenders step 120. What you have just written struck a deep chord in my heart as I "let go" of family and was taken step by step to where I live in Sydney today. Having 4 children "earth angels" to care for, the road was not always clear, but after 30 years of living this way ever increasing abundance arrives on a daily basis. Thank you for your writings. All who read them in some way are blessed, and at the age of 63, I no longer believe I am a mad woman who threw her life away, but one who has gained richness beyond compare.

Patricia Cornish
Sydney, Australia

Hello,

My heart is full of love and thankfulness for the service you are providing for us. So often I open my mailbox and find an uplifting, inspiring, or thought-provoking message that is exactly what I need at that moment. Bless you for all that you are doing. I feel blessed to have been led to you. Your messages in my mailbox have helped me to reach this place of peace. My heartfelt love to you.

God Bless,
Cathryn Green
United Kingdom

THE CODE

Intentions for a Better World
To have The Code work in your life, say it once a day

THE FIRST INTENT — SUPPORT LIFE
I refrain from opposing or harming anyone. I allow others to have their own experiences. I see life in all things and honor it as if it were my own. I support life.

THE SECOND INTENT — SEEK TRUTH
I follow my inner compass and discard any beliefs that are no longer serving me.
I go to the source. I seek truth.

THE THIRD INTENT — SET YOUR COURSE
I begin the creative process. I give direction to my life. I set my course.

THE FOURTH INTENT — SIMPLIFY
I let go so there is room for something better to come in. I intend that I am guided, guarded, protected, and lined up with the Highest Good at all times.
I trust and remain open to receive from both expected and unexpected sources. I simplify.

THE FIFTH INTENT — STAY POSITIVE
I see good, say good, and do good. I accept the gifts from all my experiences.
I am living in grace and gratitude. I stay positive.

THE SIXTH INTENT — SYNCHRONIZE
After intending and surrendering, I take action by following the opportunities that are presented to me. I am in the flow where Great Mystery and Miracles abide, fulfilling my desires and doing what I came here to do. I synchronize.

THE SEVENTH INTENT — SERVE OTHERS
I practice love in action. I always have enough to spare and enough to share.
I am available to help those who need it. I serve others.

THE EIGHTH INTENT — SHINE YOUR LIGHT
I am a magnificent being, awakening to my highest potential.
I express myself with joy, smiling easily and laughing often. I shine my light.

THE NINTH INTENT — SHARE YOUR VISION
I create my ideal world by envisioning it and telling others about it.
I share my vision.

THE TENTH INTENT — SYNERGIZE
I see Humanity as One. I enjoy gathering with light-hearted people regularly.
When we come together, we set the stage for Great Oneness to reveal itself.
We synergize.